TABLE OF CONTENTS

BREAKFAST HEROES

GAME DAY GRUB

MW00885466

MEATY MAINS

ONE POT WONDERS

SIDES AND SNACKS

DATE NIGHT DINNERS

SWEET ENDINGS

Great Recipes for Great Cooks

Cooking shouldn't be complicated. Let's face it—most of us don't have the time or patience to deal with elaborate recipes or a pile of dirty dishes. That's where this book comes in. Whether you're a guy looking to up your kitchen game or someone trying to get their husband to cook something other than microwave meals, the Crockpot for Men Cookbook is the answer. It's simple, no-frills, and packed with recipes that are as satisfying as they are easy to make.

This isn't about fancy ingredients or techniques you can't pronounce. It's about hearty, bold meals that you can throw together in minutes and let the crockpot do the work. We're talking chili that'll warm you to your core, ribs so tender they fall off the bone, and soups that'll make you feel like you've been hugged by a linebacker. This book is here to show you that cooking doesn't have to be a hassle. It's practical, foolproof, and—most importantly—delicious.

If you're a guy who thinks cooking isn't your thing, this is your chance to prove yourself wrong. If you're someone shopping for your husband, boyfriend, or that friend who's always "too busy" to cook, you're about to make their life a whole lot easier (and tastier). This isn't just a cookbook; it's a game plan for great meals with minimal effort.

With recipes that stick to the basics but deliver big flavor, this book is perfect for weeknight dinners, game-day spreads, or impressing someone without breaking a sweat. So, fire up that crockpot, grab some ingredients, and let's get cooking. You've got this—and trust us, your stomach will thank you.

> *"A man who knows his way around the kitchen doesn't just cook—he creates, he conquers, he cares."*

– Unknown

Sausage and Egg Breakfast Casserole

INGREDIENTS

- 1/2 lb breakfast sausage
- 3 large eggs
- 1 cup shredded cheddar cheese
- 1/2 cup milk
- 2 cups cubed bread

THE BENEFITS

This breakfast casserole is a high-protein meal that kickstarts your day with sustained energy. The sausage and eggs provide essential amino acids for muscle repair and strength, while the cheese contributes calcium for bone health. The milk adds additional vitamins D and B12, and the bread supplies carbs for a quick energy boost. Together, these ingredients create a balanced meal that's hearty, satisfying, and fuel-packed to keep you full throughout the morning.

PREPARATION

- Fire up your crockpot and give it a quick grease—nothing fancy, just a light coat.
- Brown up that breakfast sausage in a pan until it's cooked through. Drain off the extra grease—it's not invited.
- Grab a big bowl and whisk together your eggs and milk until it's all smooth and ready to roll.
- Toss cubed bread into the crockpot, spreading it out nice and even.
- Layer the cooked sausage right over the bread—don't skimp, make it count.
- Pour the egg mix on top, letting it soak through, then hit it with a layer of shredded cheddar.
- Cover it up and let it do its thing on low for 4–5 hours, till the eggs set and the cheese is all melty goodness.
- Sprinkle on some parsley if you're feeling fancy, then dig in!

RECIPE TIPS

Go for a sharp cheddar for a punch of flavor, or mix it up with Monterey Jack for a creamy twist. If you like spice, add chopped jalapeños or a pinch of red pepper flakes to the egg mixture. To keep it easy to clean up, use a crockpot liner. This recipe is perfect for meal prep—store leftovers in the fridge and reheat for busy mornings!

1

Overnight Cinnamon Oats

INGREDIENTS

- 1 cup rolled oats
- 1 cup almond milk (or any milk of choice)
- 1 tsp ground cinnamon
- 1 tbsp honey or maple syrup
- 1/4 cup mixed fresh berries (strawberries, blueberries)

THE BENEFITS

Overnight Cinnamon Oats offer a nutrient-packed start to your day. Rolled oats are rich in fiber, promoting digestion and heart health. Almond milk adds a dose of vitamin E and calcium, while cinnamon is known for its antioxidant properties. Honey or maple syrup provides natural sweetness with trace nutrients, and the fresh berries contribute vitamins and a burst of flavor. This easy-to-make dish balances energy and satiety, fueling you without empty calories. A powerhouse breakfast for sustained energy!

PREPARATION

- Grease your crockpot lightly so nothing sticks—don't skip this step.
- Dump in 1 cup oats, 1 cup almond milk, and 1 tsp cinnamon. Stir it up like a pro.
- Drizzle 1 tbsp honey or maple syrup over the mix for sweetness. Stir again to combine.
- Cover and set the crockpot to low. Let it cook for 6-8 hours while you sleep—no fuss.
- In the morning, stir it up, scoop into bowls, and toss on 1/4 cup berries for the win.

RECIPE TIPS

For creamier oats, mix in a splash of Greek yogurt before refrigerating. Customize toppings to suit your taste—nuts, seeds, or even dark chocolate chips work great! Want more flavor? Add vanilla extract or nutmeg to the mix. If you're running late, grab the jar and eat on the go —it's portable and mess-free. Remember, the key is to experiment with add-ins and make this recipe your own. Cooking can be fun and hassle-free—promise!

Breakfast Burrito Filling

INGREDIENTS

- 4 oz sausage (the good stuff)
- 4 large eggs
- 1/2 cup diced bell peppers (grab a mix if you're feeling fancy)
- 1/4 cup diced onion (yeah, chop it)
- 1/4 cup shredded cheddar (more if you're cheesy like that)

THE BENEFITS

This bad boy fuels you up right. Eggs bring protein and a bunch of vitamins that keep you sharp. Sausage? It's flavor-packed fuel. Peppers and onions add a punch of vitamin C and fiber to keep your engine running smooth. Cheddar seals the deal with calcium and extra protein. It's everything you need to crush your day, all in one easy, delicious breakfast.

PREPARATION

- Grease your crockpot lightly so nothing sticks—it's a game changer.
- Toss in 4 oz sausage (crumbled), 1/2 cup diced bell peppers, and 1/4 cup diced onions. Stir to mix it up.
- Crack 4 eggs into a bowl, whisk them like a champ, and pour over the sausage-veggie mix. Stir again to combine.
- Top it all with 1/4 cup shredded cheddar (or more if you're into cheese overload).
- Cover and cook on low for 2-3 hours, or until the eggs are set and everything is cooked through.
- Scoop into tortillas for burritos or eat it straight from the crockpot—no judgment here.

RECIPE TIPS

Short on time? Grab pre-cut peppers and onions—no one's judging. Want it spicy? Toss in hot sauce or diced jalapeños. Don't have cheddar? Any cheese will work—cheese is cheese, man. Make sure to heat your tortillas (microwave or skillet) so they don't crack when you wrap them up. And hey, if you mess it up, it's still eggs and sausage—it'll taste great no matter what!

French Toast Casserole

INGREDIENTS

- 4 slices of bread (any kind, but thick is best)
- 2 large eggs
- 1/2 cup milk
- 1 tbsp maple syrup (or honey, your call)
- 1/4 cup fresh berries (optional but makes it fancy)

THE BENEFITS

This French Toast Casserole fuels you with carbs for energy and protein to keep you going strong. Eggs bring vitamins D and B12, while milk packs calcium and more protein. The berries? A bonus shot of antioxidants and vitamin C. And maple syrup gives you natural sweetness with fewer regrets. It's an easy, filling, and satisfying breakfast that hits all the right notes for taste and nutrition.

PREPARATION

- Grease your crockpot—nobody likes a sticky mess.
- Rip up 4 slices of bread into chunks and toss them in. Don't overthink it, just get it done.
- In a bowl, whisk 2 eggs, 1/2 cup milk, and 1 tbsp maple syrup (or honey if that's your vibe). Pour it over the bread chunks, making sure everything gets soaked.
- Cover and cook on low for 2-3 hours, or until the egg mix is set and the bread is golden.
- Scoop it out, throw on 1/4 cup fresh berries (if you're feeling fancy), and drizzle extra syrup for good measure.

RECIPE TIPS

Use day-old bread—it soaks up the egg mix like a boss. Want it sweeter? Sprinkle some cinnamon sugar on top before baking. No berries? Bananas, nuts, or chocolate chips work just as well. Make it ahead, stash it in the fridge overnight, and just bake in the morning—boom, instant breakfast. Don't forget: a drizzle of extra syrup or a dusting of powdered sugar never hurt anyone.

Loaded Hash Browns

INGREDIENTS

- 2 cups frozen hash browns (thawed)
- 1/2 cup shredded cheddar cheese
- 2 slices crispy bacon (crumbled)
- 1/4 cup sour cream
- 2 tbsp chopped green onions

THE BENEFITS

Loaded hash browns deliver a balance of carbs for quick energy, protein from cheese and bacon, and healthy fats from sour cream. Potatoes provide potassium, supporting muscle health, while green onions add a touch of fiber and vitamins. It's comfort food with a hint of nutrition to keep you full and satisfied. Perfect for a hearty breakfast or a post-workout refuel.

PREPARATION

- Grease your crockpot to keep things slick and easy to clean.
- Toss in 2 cups of thawed hash browns and spread them out evenly—no clumps.
- Sprinkle 1/2 cup shredded cheddar cheese and 2 slices of crumbled bacon on top.
- Cover and cook on low for 2-3 hours, or until the cheese is melted and the hash browns are cooked through.
- Scoop it onto plates, top with 1/4 cup sour cream and 2 tbsp chopped green onions.

RECIPE TIPS

Want super crispy hash browns? Pat them dry before cooking—water is your enemy here. No bacon? Diced ham or leftover chicken works great. Cheese options are endless—go for mozzarella or pepper jack if cheddar isn't your vibe. Add a dash of hot sauce or jalapeños for some heat. And don't forget: cast-iron skillets make everything taste better! Keep it simple and delicious, bro.

Protein-Packed Breakfast Bowl

INGREDIENTS

- 4 large eggs
- 2 slices bacon (cooked crispy)
- 1 cup fresh spinach
- 1/2 avocado (diced)
- 1/4 cup shredded cheddar cheese

THE BENEFITS

This breakfast bowl is a power move. Eggs deliver high-quality protein and essential vitamins, while bacon adds flavor and energy. Spinach is a vitamin-rich green packed with iron, and avocado brings healthy fats to keep you full. Cheese rounds it out with calcium and extra protein. It's a balanced, satisfying meal that's perfect for fueling your workout or keeping you sharp through a busy morning.

PREPARATION

- Grease your crockpot—nobody wants eggs sticking to the sides.
- Crack 4 eggs into a bowl, whisk 'em up, and pour into the crockpot.
- Add 1 cup fresh spinach and 2 slices of crispy cooked bacon (crumbled). Stir everything together.
- Top with 1/4 cup shredded cheddar cheese and cover. Cook on low for 2-3 hours, or until the eggs are set and fluffy.
- Scoop into bowls, and finish with diced 1/2 avocado for that creamy, healthy touch.

RECIPE TIPS

Use pre-washed spinach to skip the hassle—less mess more eating. Want to switch it up? Try turkey bacon or smoked salmon instead. Keep the avocado fresh by slicing it last, and toss in some salsa if you like a little heat. No cheese? Feta or goat cheese works too. The key is layering everything in a bowl—it looks pro and tastes amazing every time.

Bacon and Cheese Strata

INGREDIENTS

- 4 oz bread (cubed, day-old works best)
- 2 slices bacon (cooked and crumbled)
- 1/2 cup shredded cheddar cheese
- 2 large eggs
- 1/2 cup milk

THE BENEFITS

This bacon and cheese strata is a protein-packed powerhouse. Eggs deliver essential nutrients like vitamin D and choline, while bacon adds flavor and energy-boosting fats. The bread provides satisfying carbs to keep you going, and cheddar cheese rounds it out with calcium and extra protein. It's a delicious way to fuel your day while enjoying comfort food vibes.

PREPARATION

- Grease your crockpot—this keeps cleanup easy and prevents sticking.
- Toss 4 oz of cubed bread into the crockpot, spreading it out evenly. Day-old bread works like a charm.
- Sprinkle in 2 slices of crumbled bacon and 1/2 cup shredded cheddar cheese.
- In a bowl, whisk 2 eggs with 1/2 cup milk, then pour the mix evenly over the bread and bacon. Give it a light press to soak everything.
- Cover and cook on low for 2-3 hours, or until the egg mixture is set and the top is golden.

RECIPE TIPS

Use stale bread—it's like a sponge for the egg mix. Want it spicier? Add a pinch of cayenne or chili flakes. If cheddar isn't your thing, swap it for mozzarella or pepper jack. Assemble it the night before, stash it in the fridge, and bake in the morning for a no-hassle breakfast. Bonus points if you pair it with a side of hot sauce or fresh greens. It's simple, hearty, and always hits the spot!

Apple Pie Oatmeal

INGREDIENTS

- 1 cup rolled oats
- 2 cups milk (or water)
- 1 medium apple (diced)
- 1 tsp ground cinnamon
- 1 tbsp maple syrup

THE BENEFITS

Apple Pie Oatmeal is packed with energy and nutrients. Rolled oats provide fiber to keep you full and aid digestion. Apples deliver natural sweetness and a hit of vitamin C. Cinnamon adds antioxidants and warmth, while maple syrup offers a touch of natural sugar without the guilt. Milk brings protein and calcium to round it out. It's a comforting, balanced breakfast that powers your day without overloading on sugar or calories.

PREPARATION

- Grease your crockpot lightly—easy cleanup is the goal.
- Toss in 1 cup rolled oats, 2 cups milk (or water), 1 diced apple, and 1 tsp ground cinnamon. Give it a solid stir to mix everything up.
- Drizzle in 1 tbsp maple syrup for a touch of sweetness, and stir again.
- Cover and cook on low for 6-8 hours overnight, letting the flavors blend into a warm, cozy breakfast.
- In the morning, stir it up, scoop into bowls, and top with extra cinnamon or a drizzle of syrup if you're feeling fancy.

RECIPE TIPS

Want it creamier? Use milk or a splash of cream at the end. No fresh apples? Go for canned or dried—they work too. Spice it up with nutmeg or a pinch of salt for more flavor. Need protein? Toss in a scoop of protein powder or a dollop of Greek yogurt on top. Don't forget: oatmeal reheats like a champ, so make extra and save yourself time tomorrow!

Buffalo Chicken Dip

INGREDIENTS

- 4 oz shredded chicken (cooked)
- 2 oz cream cheese (softened)
- 2 tbsp Buffalo sauce
- 1/4 cup shredded cheddar cheese
- 1 tbsp chopped green onions

THE BENEFITS

This Buffalo Chicken Dip is a flavor-packed, protein-rich snack. The shredded chicken provides lean protein for muscle repair, while cheddar cheese and cream cheese add calcium and healthy fats. Buffalo sauce spices things up with a kick, and green onions bring in a touch of vitamins. Paired with veggies or chips, it's a satisfying dip that hits the balance between indulgence and nutrition. Perfect for game day or anytime snacking!

PREPARATION

- Grease your crockpot—makes cleanup a breeze.
- Toss in 4 oz shredded chicken, 2 oz softened cream cheese, and 2 tbsp Buffalo sauce. Give it a solid mix to combine everything.
- Sprinkle 1/4 cup shredded cheddar cheese over the top—don't skimp!
- Cover and cook on low for 1-2 hours, stirring halfway through to make it extra creamy.
- Top with 1 tbsp chopped green onions for that finishing touch.

RECIPE TIPS

Use rotisserie chicken for extra flavor and less work. Want it spicier? Add a dash of hot sauce or cayenne. Prefer it creamier? Stir in a little ranch or blue cheese dressing. Make it a crowd-pleaser by doubling the recipe, and keep it warm in a small slow cooker. Tortilla chips, celery sticks, or even breadsticks work great as dippers—go wild with the sides! Simple, quick, and always a hit.

Pulled Pork Sliders

INGREDIENTS

- 6 slider buns
- 4 oz pulled pork (cooked and shredded)
- 2 tbsp barbecue sauce
- 1/4 cup coleslaw mix
- 1 tbsp mayonnaise

THE BENEFITS

Pulled Pork Sliders combine protein-packed pork with a dose of fiber and crunch from coleslaw. Pork provides essential nutrients like zinc and iron, while barbecue sauce adds flavor without overloading on calories (in moderation). The coleslaw mix brings a hit of vitamin C, and slider buns provide energy-boosting carbs. These sliders are satisfying, flavorful, and balanced enough to power your day without slowing you down.

PREPARATION

- Prep your crockpot with a light grease to avoid sticking.
- Add 4 oz of pulled pork and mix in 2 tbsp barbecue sauce. Give it a toss so the sauce coats the pork nicely.
- Cover and let it warm up on low for 1-2 hours while the flavors mingle.
- In a separate bowl, stir together 1/4 cup coleslaw mix with 1 tbsp mayo for a simple crunchy topping.
- Lightly toast 6 slider buns, stack the pulled pork, add a dollop of slaw, and close them up.

RECIPE TIPS

Use leftover pork for maximum convenience—it's already packed with flavor. Want to spice things up? Add jalapeño slices or a dash of hot sauce. Prefer a tangier slaw? Mix in a little vinegar with the mayo. Toasting the buns keeps them from getting soggy, so don't skip that step. Serve with a side of chips or pickles to complete the experience. Simple, tasty, and guaranteed to impress!

Spicy Queso Dip

INGREDIENTS

- 4 oz Velveeta cheese (cubed)
- 1/4 cup milk
- 1 tbsp diced jalapeños (fresh or jarred)
- 1/4 tsp smoked paprika
- Tortilla chips (for dipping)

THE BENEFITS

Spicy Queso Dip brings a dose of comfort with a touch of spice. Velveeta provides calcium and protein in every creamy bite, while jalapeños add vitamins A and C along with metabolism-boosting capsaicin. The milk enhances creaminess and delivers essential nutrients like vitamin D. Pairing it with tortilla chips gives you the crunch and energy boost you need to enjoy every bite. This quick, satisfying snack hits all the right spots!

PREPARATION

- Cut 4 oz Velveeta into chunks and drop them into the crockpot.
- Pour in 1/4 cup milk, then sprinkle with 1 tbsp diced jalapeños and 1/4 tsp smoked paprika for that extra kick.
- Set the crockpot to low and let the cheese melt, stirring occasionally to keep things smooth and creamy.
- Once fully melted, give it a final stir to mix everything evenly.
- Serve straight from the crockpot with a heap of tortilla chips on the side—no mess, all flavor.

RECIPE TIPS

Keep the cheese from hardening by serving it in a small slow cooker or over a warming tray. Want it spicier? Add hot sauce or a pinch of cayenne. Prefer a milder vibe? Swap jalapeños for diced green chilies. If you're out of paprika, chili powder works too. Don't forget to mix often while heating—it's the secret to silky, smooth queso. Add diced tomatoes or cooked sausage for a heartier version. Simple and endlessly customizable!

Honey Garlic Meatballs

INGREDIENTS

- 8 oz ground meat (beef or chicken)
- 2 tbsp breadcrumbs
- 1 tbsp honey
- 1 tbsp soy sauce
- 1 garlic clove (minced)

THE BENEFITS

Honey Garlic Meatballs pack protein from the meat, helping you build and repair muscles. Garlic brings a hit of antioxidants and immune-boosting benefits, while honey provides natural sweetness with a dose of energy. Soy sauce adds flavor without piling on calories, and breadcrumbs keep the meatballs tender and satisfying. Pair with rice or veggies for a balanced meal that's full of flavor and keeps you going strong!

PREPARATION

- In a bowl, mix 8 oz ground meat with 2 tbsp breadcrumbs and 1 minced garlic clove. Roll into bite-sized meatballs.
- Place the meatballs in the crockpot, spreading them out in a single layer.
- In a small bowl, combine 1 tbsp honey and 1 tbsp soy sauce, then pour the mixture over the meatballs.
- Cover and cook on low for 3-4 hours, letting the sauce soak into the meatballs for that sweet and savory kick.
- Serve directly from the crockpot, and watch them disappear—perfect for snacking or as a main dish!

RECIPE TIPS

Want a juicier bite? Use a mix of ground beef and pork. No breadcrumbs? Crushed crackers work just fine. Double the sauce if you're a dipper—it's worth it. For easy rolling, wet your hands to prevent sticking. Add a touch of chili flakes to the sauce if you like it spicy. Serve over steamed rice, noodles, or even a bed of greens to level up your presentation. Simple, quick, and always a winner!

Chili Cheese Fries Base

INGREDIENTS

- 8 oz frozen fries
- 1/2 cup canned chili (warmed)
- 1/4 cup shredded cheddar cheese
- 1 tbsp chopped green onions
- 1 tbsp sour cream (optional)

THE BENEFITS

Chili Cheese Fries deliver energy-packed carbs from the fries and protein from the chili and cheese. Cheddar provides calcium for strong bones, while green onions add a touch of fiber and vitamins. Sour cream is an optional indulgence that adds richness without going overboard. This dish combines flavor, texture, and essential nutrients in a way that satisfies hunger and keeps you fueled for hours. Perfect for a casual meal or a game-day treat!

PREPARATION

- Preheat your oven and bake 8 oz of frozen fries until crispy—don't skimp on the crunch.
- While the fries bake, pour 1/2 cup canned chili into the crockpot and set it to low to keep warm.
- Once the fries are ready, transfer them to the crockpot and layer them with the warm chili.
- Sprinkle 1/4 cup shredded cheddar cheese on top, cover, and let it melt for about 5 minutes.
- Serve topped with 1 tbsp chopped green onions and a dollop of sour cream if you're feeling fancy.

RECIPE TIPS

Want crispier fries? Flip them halfway through baking. Prefer spicier chili? Add a dash of hot sauce or some diced jalapeños. For extra cheesiness, layer fries and chili in a dish, sprinkle cheese, and broil until it melts. No green onions? Diced red onions work too. Make it heartier by adding toppings like crumbled bacon or a fried egg. Serve hot and enjoy—it's best when fresh out of the oven!

Teriyaki Chicken Wings

INGREDIENTS

- 8 chicken wings
- 2 tbsp teriyaki sauce
- 1 tbsp soy sauce
- 1 tsp sesame seeds
- 1 tbsp chopped green onions

THE BENEFITS

This bacon and cheese strata is a protein-packed powerhouse. Eggs deliver essential nutrients like vitamin D and choline, while bacon adds flavor and energy-boosting fats. The bread provides satisfying carbs to keep you going, and cheddar cheese rounds it out with calcium and extra protein. It's a delicious way to fuel your day while enjoying comfort food vibes.

PREPARATION

- Toss 8 chicken wings into the crockpot—no need for fancy prep, just get them in there.
- Mix 2 tbsp teriyaki sauce and 1 tbsp soy sauce in a small bowl, then pour it over the wings. Stir to coat everything evenly.
- Cover and cook on low for 3-4 hours, letting the wings soak up all that sweet, savory goodness.
- Once cooked, sprinkle 1 tsp sesame seeds and 1 tbsp chopped green onions on top for extra flair.
- Plate 'em up and dive in—perfectly glazed and bursting with flavor.

RECIPE TIPS

Use stale bread—it's like a sponge for the egg mix. Want it spicier? Add a pinch of cayenne or chili flakes. If cheddar isn't your thing, swap it for mozzarella or pepper jack. Assemble it the night before, stash it in the fridge, and bake in the morning for a no-hassle breakfast. Bonus points if you pair it with a side of hot sauce or fresh greens. It's simple, hearty, and always hits the spot!

Loaded Nacho Dip

INGREDIENTS

- 4 oz ground beef (browned)
- 4 oz Velveeta cheese (cubed)
- 1/4 cup diced tomatoes
- 1 tbsp diced jalapeños
- Tortilla chips (for dipping)

THE BENEFITS

This Loaded Nacho Dip offers a satisfying mix of protein, fats, and flavor. Ground beef provides essential protein for muscle repair, while Velveeta cheese adds calcium and energy-boosting fats. Tomatoes bring a dose of vitamin C and antioxidants, and jalapeños add metabolism-boosting capsaicin. Pair it with tortilla chips for a carb boost, making it a complete, hearty snack that's perfect for parties or lazy nights in.

PREPARATION

- Brown 4 oz ground beef in a skillet, then drain the grease.
- Grease your crockpot lightly and toss in the browned beef and 4 oz Velveeta cheese cubes.
- Add 1/4 cup diced tomatoes and 1 tbsp diced jalapeños for a flavorful punch. Stir to combine.
- Cover and cook on low for 1-2 hours, stirring occasionally, until the cheese is fully melted and everything is mixed perfectly.
- Serve straight from the crockpot with a big bowl of tortilla chips. It's hot, cheesy, and guaranteed to impress.

RECIPE TIPS

Want more spice? Add a dash of hot sauce or extra jalapeños. If Velveeta isn't your thing, swap in shredded cheddar or pepper jack for a sharper flavor. Stir occasionally while it cooks to prevent any clumping. For extra flair, garnish the finished dip with chopped cilantro or green onions. This dip pairs perfectly with a cold drink and your favorite movie or game—dig in and enjoy!

Beer Brats with Onions

INGREDIENTS

- 2 bratwurst sausages
- 1 cup beer (lager works best)
- 1/2 large onion (sliced)
- 2 tbsp mustard (for serving)
- 2 buns (toasted)

THE BENEFITS

Beer Brats with Onions deliver protein from the bratwurst and antioxidants from the onions. Cooking with beer not only enhances the flavor but also adds trace nutrients like B vitamins. Using mustard keeps the calorie count in check while adding bold flavor. Paired with a whole-grain bun, this meal provides energy and satisfaction without unnecessary guilt. It's a balanced, indulgent option perfect for game day or casual dining.

PREPARATION

- Place 2 bratwurst sausages and 1/2 sliced onion into the crockpot.
- Pour in 1 cup of beer, making sure the brats are submerged halfway.
- Cover and cook on low for 4-5 hours, letting the flavors soak into the sausages.
- Once done, toast 2 buns and load them with the brats and onions. Add 2 tbsp mustard (or your favorite topping) for an extra kick.
- Serve hot, grab a cold beer, and enjoy this hearty meal!

RECIPE TIPS

For extra caramelization, sear the brats in a skillet before tossing them into the crockpot. Don't have beer? Substitute chicken broth or apple cider for a different flavor. Want a spicier twist? Use jalapeño mustard or add chili flakes. Serve with sauerkraut or pickles for added crunch and tang. Keep the buns warm in foil if you're not eating right away—nobody likes cold bread! This is the ultimate no-fuss comfort food.

Slow-Cooked Chili

INGREDIENTS

- 8 oz ground beef
- 1/2 cup canned beans (kidney or black)
- 1/2 cup canned diced tomatoes
- 1 tsp chili powder
- 1/4 cup shredded cheddar cheese

THE BENEFITS

This Slow-Cooked Chili brings a powerful blend of protein, fiber, and flavor. Ground beef is packed with protein and iron, keeping you strong and energized. Beans add fiber and essential nutrients, aiding digestion and keeping you full longer. Tomatoes bring antioxidants and a dose of vitamin C. Topped with cheddar cheese for calcium, this hearty dish fuels you up for whatever comes your way. Simple, nutritious, and undeniably satisfying!

PREPARATION

- Toss 8 oz of ground beef into a skillet, cook until browned, and drain the grease.
- Add the cooked beef, 1/2 cup beans, 1/2 cup diced tomatoes, and 1 tsp chili powder into the crockpot. Stir it up for good measure.
- Cover and cook on low for 4-5 hours, letting the flavors meld into a hearty, rich chili.
- When done, ladle into bowls, top each with 1/4 cup shredded cheddar cheese, and enjoy! Add sour cream or green onions if you're feeling extra.

RECIPE TIPS

Use lean ground beef to keep it lighter without losing the flavor. Want a spicier chili? Add a pinch of cayenne or diced jalapeños. For a smoky twist, throw in some smoked paprika or chipotle powder. Serve with cornbread or tortilla chips for extra crunch. Leftovers? They freeze and reheat like a dream, so make a big batch. A slow-cooked winner every time!

Beef Bourguignon

INGREDIENTS

- 8 oz beef chuck (cubed)
- 1/2 cup red wine
- 1/2 cup sliced mushrooms
- 1/4 cup diced carrots
- 1 tsp minced garlic

THE BENEFITS

Beef Bourguignon is a hearty dish packed with protein and essential nutrients. Beef chuck delivers iron and B vitamins for energy and muscle repair. Carrots and mushrooms add fiber, antioxidants, and vitamins for overall health. The red wine enhances flavor and provides a dose of heart-healthy antioxidants. This slow-cooked classic is a comforting meal that nourishes while satisfying your hunger.

PREPARATION

- Grease your crockpot to keep cleanup easy. Toss in 8 oz of cubed beef chuck, 1/2 cup sliced mushrooms, and 1/4 cup diced carrots.
- Pour 1/2 cup red wine over the ingredients, then add 1 tsp minced garlic for that bold flavor. Stir to combine.
- Cover and cook on low for 6-8 hours, letting the beef turn tender and the flavors meld into a rich sauce.
- Serve it up hot, garnished with fresh parsley, and pair with crusty bread or mashed potatoes.

RECIPE TIPS

Sear the beef in a skillet before adding it to the crockpot for extra flavor. Use a dry red wine like Cabernet Sauvignon for the best taste. If you don't have red wine, beef broth works as a substitute. Add potatoes or pearl onions if you want to bulk it up. Serve with crusty bread to soak up that rich sauce—it's comfort food at its finest!

BBQ Pulled Pork

INGREDIENTS

- 8 oz pork shoulder (boneless, trimmed)
- 1/2 cup barbecue sauce
- 1/4 cup chicken broth
- 1 tbsp brown sugar
- 2 slider buns or bread rolls

THE BENEFITS

BBQ Pulled Pork is a protein-packed dish that's both flavorful and satisfying. Pork shoulder provides a healthy dose of protein and essential nutrients like iron and zinc. Barbecue sauce and brown sugar add a touch of sweetness, while chicken broth keeps it moist without unnecessary fat. Pair it with whole-grain buns or a side salad for a balanced, hearty meal. This classic comfort food is as nutritious as it is delicious!

PREPARATION

- Place 8 oz pork shoulder into the crockpot. Pour in 1/4 cup chicken broth to keep it juicy.
- Add 1/2 cup barbecue sauce and 1 tbsp brown sugar over the pork, ensuring it's coated evenly.
- Cover and cook on low for 6-8 hours, letting the pork get tender enough to shred.
- Once cooked, shred the pork using two forks right in the crockpot, mixing it with the sauce.
- Serve on slider buns or rolls with your favorite toppings like coleslaw or pickles.

RECIPE TIPS

Sear the pork before putting it in the crockpot for an extra layer of flavor. Prefer a tangy kick? Add a splash of apple cider vinegar to the mix. Leftovers can be stored in the fridge and taste even better the next day. Serve with coleslaw or a side of pickles for crunch. Toast the buns lightly for a sturdy base that won't get soggy. Effortless and full of flavor!

Garlic Herb Chicken Thighs

INGREDIENTS

- 2 chicken thighs (bone-in, skin-on)
- 1 tbsp olive oil
- 1 tsp minced garlic
- 1 tsp dried herbs (thyme, rosemary, or your favorite mix)
- 1/4 tsp salt

THE BENEFITS

Garlic Herb Chicken Thighs are a protein powerhouse, perfect for muscle repair and sustained energy. The olive oil provides heart-healthy fats, while garlic and herbs pack antioxidants and anti-inflammatory benefits. Bone-in chicken retains moisture and adds iron and zinc to your diet. With no processed ingredients, this dish is wholesome, flavorful, and nutritious, making it an excellent choice for a filling, healthy meal.

PREPARATION

- Grease your crockpot lightly with 1 tbsp olive oil to prevent sticking.
- Season 2 chicken thighs with 1/4 tsp salt, 1 tsp minced garlic, and 1 tsp dried herbs. Rub it in to coat evenly.
- Place the thighs in the crockpot, skin side up, so they crisp up nicely.
- Cover and cook on low for 4-5 hours until the chicken is tender and cooked through.
- Serve hot, garnished with fresh herbs, alongside roasted veggies or mashed potatoes for a full meal.

RECIPE TIPS

Pat the chicken thighs dry before seasoning for extra crispy skin. For more flavor, sear the thighs in a skillet before adding them to the crockpot. Want a citrusy kick? Add a squeeze of lemon juice before serving. Toss some root vegetables in the crockpot with the chicken for a one-pot meal. Leftovers make for killer sandwiches or salads the next day. Easy, tasty, and built for maximum flavor!

Garlic Herb Chicken Thighs

INGREDIENTS

- 1 lb chicken thighs (bone-in, skin-on)
- 2 tbsp olive oil
- 1 tsp garlic powder
- 1 tsp dried thyme
- 1/2 tsp salt

THE BENEFITS

This recipe is a protein powerhouse, perfect for muscle repair and energy. The olive oil delivers healthy fats, supporting heart health, while garlic and thyme bring antioxidants. With no heavy creams or added sugars, this dish keeps calories balanced and nutrients high, ideal for anyone aiming to eat clean without sacrificing flavor.

PREPARATION

- Rub those chicken thighs with olive oil like you're giving them a massage—don't skimp, they need it.
- Sprinkle on the garlic powder, thyme, and salt like you're seasoning a steak—generously and evenly.
- Heat up a skillet on medium-high, then slap those thighs skin-side down for about 3 minutes to get that golden sear.
- Flip 'em over and give the other side a quick touch-up—just enough to seal the deal.
- Toss the thighs into your crockpot, skin-side up, because presentation matters.
- Set the crockpot to high for 3-4 hours, or go low and slow for 6-8 hours.
- Want crispy skin? Hit them under the broiler for 3 minutes after they're done.
- Plate up and garnish with some fresh herbs—makes you look like a pro. Dig in!

RECIPE TIPS

For the best flavor, marinate the chicken thighs with herbs and oil overnight—it's a game-changer! Use skin-on thighs for that golden, crispy finish. Got leftovers? Shred the chicken and toss it into a salad or tacos. Don't skip the skillet sear—it locks in juices and adds a crispy layer. If you're short on time, use a slow-cooker liner to minimize cleanup. Keep an eye on liquid levels—if you like a saucier finish, add a splash of broth before cooking.

Beef and Sweet Potato Stew

INGREDIENTS

- 3/4 lb beef stew meat
- 1 medium sweet potato (about 10 oz), diced
- 1 cup beef broth
- 1 tbsp tomato paste
- 1 tsp dried thyme

THE BENEFITS

Packed with protein, iron, and vitamins, this stew is both filling and nutritious. Beef fuels muscle repair and boosts energy, while sweet potatoes deliver fiber, Vitamin A, and natural sweetness. Tomato paste adds antioxidants, and thyme brings in a dose of immune-boosting goodness. With minimal fats and no refined carbs, it's a guilt-free comfort food ideal for keeping you fueled and satisfied.

PREPARATION

- Cut the beef into bite-sized chunks if needed. Toss them into a hot skillet for a quick sear—don't skip this, it's where the flavor starts.
- Peel and dice the sweet potato into hearty chunks—something you'd want on your spoon.
- Layer the beef and sweet potato in your crockpot like you're building a tasty fortress.
- Stir the beef broth, tomato paste, and thyme in a small bowl until combined. Pour this over the beef and potatoes.
- Cover the crockpot, set it to low for 6-8 hours, or high for 4 hours—then forget about it.
- Once done, give it a quick stir, ladle into bowls, and sprinkle with fresh parsley if you're feeling fancy.

RECIPE TIPS

Give the beef a proper sear before it hits the crockpot—this step adds killer flavor. Use fresh thyme if you've got it; it'll make the dish even more fragrant. If you like a thicker broth, mash a few sweet potato chunks into the mix before serving. Don't over-stir while cooking, though—you want those beef pieces to stay tender. Leftovers? This stew tastes even better the next day.

Honey Mustard Pork Loin

INGREDIENTS

- 1 lb pork loin
- 2 tbsp honey
- 2 tbsp Dijon mustard
- 1 tsp garlic powder
- 1/2 tsp salt

THE BENEFITS

This recipe combines lean protein and healthy carbs for a balanced meal. Pork loin is low in fat but packed with protein, essential for muscle building and repair. Honey provides natural sweetness and energy without refined sugars, while Dijon mustard adds flavor without extra calories. Garlic powder boosts immunity, and the simple ingredients keep it clean and nutritious.

PREPARATION

- Pat the pork loin dry with paper towels, then rub it down with garlic powder and salt—don't be shy.
- Mix honey and Dijon mustard in a small bowl until smooth—this is your sauce of glory.
- Heat a skillet on medium-high, sear the pork loin for 2-3 minutes per side to lock in flavor.
- Place the pork in the crockpot and pour your honey mustard mix all over it like you mean it.
- Cover and cook on low for 6-7 hours or high for 3-4 hours.
- Slice it up and drizzle with the extra sauce from the pot. Serve it up with roasted veggies or a salad if you're feeling ambitious.

RECIPE TIPS

Always sear the pork first—it's the secret to locking in those juices. Use a meat thermometer to avoid overcooking; aim for 145°F. Got leftover sauce in the crockpot? Drizzle it over roasted veggies or mashed potatoes. Prefer a sweeter kick? Add a splash of apple cider vinegar to the sauce. This dish is great for meal prep —slice and store for quick sandwiches or salads.

Chicken and Dumplings

INGREDIENTS

- 1/2 lb chicken breast, diced
- 1 cup chicken broth
- 1/2 cup all-purpose flour
- 1/4 cup milk
- 1/2 tsp garlic powder

THE BENEFITS

This recipe packs lean protein from the chicken to fuel muscle repair and keep you satisfied. Chicken broth is hydrating and full of collagen, great for your joints and skin. The dumplings are a hearty source of carbohydrates, providing energy without overloading on processed ingredients. With garlic powder boosting immunity, this dish is a balanced, nutrient-rich comfort meal that feels indulgent without being heavy.

PREPARATION

- Dice the chicken into bite-sized pieces like you mean business.
- Heat a skillet and give the chicken a quick sear—just enough to get it golden, then toss it into your crockpot.
- Pour in the chicken broth and sprinkle in garlic powder for that extra kick. Stir it all up.
- In a bowl, mix flour, milk, and a pinch of salt to make a sticky dumpling dough.
- Drop spoonfuls of the dough right on top of the chicken mix in the crockpot—don't worry, they'll puff up.
- Cover and cook on low for 5-6 hours or high for 3-4 hours.
- When it's done, fluff the dumplings a bit with a fork, plate up, and sprinkle with fresh parsley.

RECIPE TIPS

Sear the chicken first for extra flavor—it's worth the extra step. Use cold milk for the dumplings to make them fluffier. Don't open the crockpot while cooking; the dumplings need that steam to rise. Want extra flavor? Add a bay leaf or some thyme to the broth. Leftovers? They reheat like a dream, but add a splash of broth when warming to keep everything moist.

Teriyaki Beef Bowls

INGREDIENTS

- 1/2 lb beef strips
- 1/4 cup teriyaki sauce
- 1 cup cooked white rice
- 1 cup broccoli florets
- 1 tsp sesame seeds

THE BENEFITS

This dish balances lean beef for muscle-building protein with broccoli, a Vitamin C-packed vegetable great for immunity and digestion. Teriyaki sauce provides a flavorful but modest calorie addition, while sesame seeds bring healthy fats and minerals like calcium. The white rice delivers energy-boosting carbs to keep you going. This simple, wholesome bowl checks all the boxes for a satisfying, nutrient-rich meal.

PREPARATION

- Slice the beef into thin strips if it isn't already prepped.
- Heat a skillet and sear the beef for 2 minutes on each side for that charred flavor. Add to your crockpot.
- Pour the teriyaki sauce over the beef, ensuring it's evenly coated.
- Add the broccoli florets on top for easy steaming as the beef cooks.
- Cover and cook on low for 4-5 hours or high for 2-3 hours.
- Fluff up your cooked white rice and divide it into two bowls.
- Scoop the teriyaki beef and broccoli onto the rice, making sure to drizzle some of the sauce from the pot.
- Sprinkle sesame seeds and chopped green onions (if you've got them) for garnish.

RECIPE TIPS

Go for thinly sliced beef to soak up the teriyaki sauce. Prefer a richer flavor? Add a splash of soy sauce or ginger. Don't skip the skillet sear—it locks in juices and adds depth. Use a rice cooker for perfect rice without the fuss. Want a crunch? Toast the sesame seeds before sprinkling. Broccoli can overcook—add it halfway through if you like it firmer. Leftovers? These bowls heat up like a charm for a quick next-day meal.

Lemon Garlic Chicken Breasts

INGREDIENTS

- 2 chicken breasts (about 1 lb)
- 2 tbsp lemon juice
- 1 tsp garlic powder
- 1/2 tsp salt
- 1/4 cup chicken broth

THE BENEFITS

This recipe is a clean and lean protein-packed meal that's big on flavor and low on guilt. Chicken breasts provide essential protein with minimal fat, while garlic powder adds an immune-boosting punch. Lemon juice brings Vitamin C for skin and immunity, and chicken broth hydrates while delivering vital nutrients. With only five simple ingredients, this dish is a nutritional powerhouse that satisfies cravings without unnecessary calories or processed ingredients.

PREPARATION

- Pat the chicken breasts dry with paper towels, then sprinkle with garlic powder and salt on both sides.
- Heat a skillet over medium-high heat and sear the chicken for 2 minutes per side to get a golden crust.
- Place the chicken in your crockpot, laying them flat for even cooking.
- Mix the lemon juice and chicken broth in a small bowl, then pour it over the chicken in the crockpot.
- Cover and cook on low for 4-5 hours or high for 2-3 hours until the chicken is juicy and tender.
- Once done, spoon some of the sauce from the pot over the chicken for extra flavor.
- Garnish with fresh parsley and lemon slices if you're feeling fancy. Serve with veggies or rice.

RECIPE TIPS

Sear the chicken first for maximum flavor—it's worth the extra two minutes. Use fresh lemon juice for the best zingy flavor. Want even more sauce? Add a little extra chicken broth or a touch of olive oil. Don't overcook—check for an internal temp of 165°F. For variety, throw in some baby potatoes or green beans with the chicken. Leftovers? Shred the chicken and use it in salads or wraps the next day!

Hearty Beef Stew

INGREDIENTS

- 3/4 lb beef stew meat
- 1 medium potato (about 8 oz), diced
- 1 medium carrot (about 6 oz), sliced
- 1 cup beef broth
- 1 tsp dried thyme

THE BENEFITS

This beef stew is loaded with protein, essential for muscle repair and satiety. The hearty beef chunks are paired with fiber-rich carrots and potassium-packed potatoes, creating a balanced meal. Beef broth is hydrating and full of minerals that support joint and skin health. Low in processed ingredients, this dish provides essential vitamins and antioxidants from its simple yet wholesome components, making it a nutrient-dense comfort food.

PREPARATION

- Chop the beef into bite-sized chunks if needed. Sear them in a hot skillet for a couple of minutes to lock in flavor, then toss them into your crockpot.
- Dice the potato and slice the carrot into hearty chunks. Add these to the pot—don't skimp, it's stew, after all.
- Pour in the beef broth and sprinkle with thyme for that herby kick. Stir it up for even flavor distribution.
- Cover and cook on low for 6-8 hours or high for 3-4 hours. The longer, the better.
- When it's done, give it a quick stir and serve hot, garnished with fresh parsley if you want to look fancy. Pair with crusty bread for dunking.

RECIPE TIPS

Searing the beef first adds depth to the stew—don't skip it. If you prefer a thicker stew, mash a few potato chunks before serving. Add a splash of red wine or Worcestershire sauce to the broth for a flavor boost. Stir in some frozen peas in the last 30 minutes for extra color and nutrition. This stew tastes even better the next day, so make extra for easy meal prep!

Herb-Crusted Pork Roast

INGREDIENTS

- 1 lb pork loin roast
- 1 tsp dried rosemary
- 1 tsp dried thyme
- 1/2 tsp garlic powder
- 1/2 tsp salt

THE BENEFITS

This herb-crusted pork roast is a lean protein powerhouse, perfect for muscle repair and long-lasting energy. Rosemary and thyme aren't just flavorful—they're loaded with antioxidants that fight inflammation. Garlic powder adds an immune-boosting punch, while the minimal use of salt keeps it heart-healthy. This recipe is a clean, wholesome way to enjoy a comforting meal with natural flavors and essential nutrients for your active lifestyle.

PREPARATION

- Pat the pork roast dry with paper towels to help the seasoning stick better.
- Mix rosemary, thyme, garlic powder, and salt in a small bowl. Rub this herb mix all over the pork—be generous.
- Heat a skillet on medium-high and sear the pork for about 2 minutes on each side to get a nice crust.
- Transfer the pork to your crockpot and cover it. Cook on low for 6-7 hours or high for 3-4 hours.
- Once done, let the roast rest for 5 minutes before slicing—it'll be juicier this way.
- Plate the slices and drizzle any juices from the crockpot over the top. Serve with veggies or potatoes for a hearty meal.

RECIPE TIPS

Sear the pork first—it locks in the juices and gives a golden crust. Want a stronger herb flavor? Use fresh rosemary and thyme instead of dried. Don't skip the resting step after cooking; it makes slicing easier and keeps the pork tender. If you're craving more sauce, deglaze the skillet with a splash of chicken broth after searing. Leftovers? This roast is perfect for sandwiches or salads the next day.

Creamy Ranch Chicken

INGREDIENTS

- 2 chicken breasts (about 1 lb)
- 1/2 cup ranch dressing
- 1/4 cup chicken broth
- 1 tsp garlic powder
- 1/4 cup shredded cheddar cheese

THE BENEFITS

This dish combines protein-rich chicken with a modest amount of creamy ranch sauce for satisfying comfort. Chicken breasts provide lean protein for muscle repair, while cheddar cheese adds a touch of calcium and flavor. Using garlic powder and ranch dressing brings taste without overloading on calories or unnecessary fats. Balanced with a simple carb side like potatoes or rice, this recipe delivers essential nutrients in a hearty, family-friendly package.

PREPARATION

- Pat the chicken breasts dry and sprinkle with garlic powder on both sides—season like you mean it.
- Heat a skillet and sear the chicken for 2 minutes per side to get a golden crust. Toss it into your crockpot.
- In a bowl, mix ranch dressing and chicken broth until smooth. Pour this creamy goodness over the chicken in the crockpot.
- Cover and cook on low for 4-5 hours or high for 2-3 hours—let the flavors do their magic.
- About 30 minutes before it's done, sprinkle the cheddar cheese on top and let it melt into the sauce.
- Serve the chicken smothered in the creamy sauce with sides like mashed potatoes or rice. Garnish with parsley for bonus points.

RECIPE TIPS

Sear the chicken for a flavor boost before adding it to the crockpot. Don't skip the cheese—it makes the sauce extra indulgent. Use low-sodium chicken broth to keep things healthy without sacrificing taste. For a kick, add a pinch of red pepper flakes to the ranch mix. Leftovers? Shred the chicken and use it for sandwiches or wraps. Always let the chicken rest for a few minutes before serving—it locks in the juiciness.

Chicken Alfredo Pasta

INGREDIENTS

- 1/2 lb chicken breast, sliced
- 1/2 lb fettuccine pasta
- 1 cup Alfredo sauce
- 1/4 cup grated Parmesan cheese
- 1 tsp garlic powder

THE BENEFITS

This Chicken Alfredo Pasta balances lean protein, carbs, and healthy fats for a satisfying meal. Chicken breast delivers high-quality protein, essential for muscle growth and repair. The Alfredo sauce provides healthy fats and calcium, while Parmesan cheese adds flavor without overwhelming calories. Fettuccine pasta serves as a great energy source, and garlic powder offers subtle immune-boosting benefits. It's an indulgent yet balanced dish perfect for refueling after a long day.

PREPARATION

- Slice the chicken breast into strips—nice and even for easy cooking. Sprinkle with garlic powder for extra flavor.
- Heat a skillet over medium heat and sear the chicken for 3 minutes per side until golden. Set aside.
- Cook the fettuccine pasta according to the package instructions. Drain and set it aside.
- In your crockpot, add the Alfredo sauce and cooked pasta. Stir to coat the pasta evenly.
- Layer the cooked chicken strips on top of the pasta. Sprinkle with Parmesan cheese.
- Cover and cook on low for 2 hours to let the flavors combine.
- Serve it up, garnished with fresh parsley and more Parmesan if you like. Pair it with garlic bread for the win.

RECIPE TIPS

Sear the chicken for a flavorful crust before tossing it into the crockpot. To prevent pasta from getting mushy, undercook it slightly before adding it to the sauce. Use fresh Parmesan for a sharper, creamier finish. Add a pinch of nutmeg to the Alfredo sauce for an extra flavor kick. This dish is great for leftovers—just add a splash of milk when reheating to revive the creamy sauce!

Loaded Mac and Cheese

INGREDIENTS

- 1 cup elbow macaroni
- 1 cup shredded cheddar cheese
- 1/2 cup milk
- 2 strips bacon, cooked and crumbled
- 1 tbsp green onions, chopped

THE BENEFITS

Loaded Mac and Cheese combines protein from cheese and bacon with energy-boosting carbs from pasta. The milk adds calcium for strong bones, while green onions provide a hint of Vitamin C and antioxidants. With minimal processed ingredients, this dish offers a fun balance of indulgence and nutrition in every bite, satisfying your craving for comfort food without overloading on unhealthy fats.

PREPARATION

- Cook the elbow macaroni according to package instructions. Drain and set aside.
- Toss your cooked pasta into the crockpot. Add the shredded cheddar and pour in the milk. Stir it up until it's evenly mixed.
- Set the crockpot on low and let it cook for 1.5-2 hours, stirring occasionally to keep the cheese from clumping.
- Meanwhile, cook up two strips of bacon in a skillet until crispy, then crumble them like a pro.
- When the mac and cheese is gooey and creamy, sprinkle the bacon bits and chopped green onions over the top for that loaded magic.
- Scoop it into bowls, add a little extra cheddar if you're feeling bold.

RECIPE TIPS

Cook the pasta just shy of done—it'll finish in the crockpot and soak up all that cheesy goodness. Crispy bacon is key, so don't rush it; use paper towels to soak up extra grease. Stir occasionally to prevent sticking and ensure even melting. For extra flavor, mix in a dash of garlic powder or a splash of hot sauce. Got leftovers? Reheat with a splash of milk to keep it creamy. This is comfort food at its best—go all in!

Vegetable Curry

INGREDIENTS

- 1 medium potato (about 8 oz), diced
- 1/2 cup carrots, sliced
- 1/2 cup bell peppers, diced
- 1 cup coconut milk
- 2 tsp curry powder

THE BENEFITS

This vegetable curry is a nutrient-packed dish loaded with vitamins, fiber, and antioxidants. The carrots and bell peppers bring Vitamin A and C, boosting immunity and eye health. Potatoes provide energy-sustaining carbs and potassium, while coconut milk offers healthy fats that support heart health and digestion. Curry powder adds anti-inflammatory benefits, making this a flavorful, well-rounded meal. It's a plant-based powerhouse perfect for fueling your day.

PREPARATION

- Chop up the potato, carrots, and bell peppers into bite-sized pieces—nothing too fancy, just manageable chunks.
- Throw the veggies into your crockpot. No need to layer; just pile them in.
- Mix the curry powder into the coconut milk until it's a golden, fragrant sauce. Pour it over the vegetables, ensuring everything gets a nice coat.
- Cover the crockpot, set it to low for 6 hours or high for 3 hours, and let it do the work. Stir once or twice if you're around.
- When it's done, the veggies should be tender and the curry thick and creamy.
- Serve it up with rice or naan bread on the side. Garnish with fresh cilantro.

RECIPE TIPS

Cut the veggies into equal sizes so they cook evenly. Want more protein? Add chickpeas or tofu. Don't skip the coconut milk—it's the key to that rich, creamy texture. For extra heat, toss in some red chili flakes or diced jalapeño. Stir the curry halfway through cooking to keep the flavors mixed. If you're in a rush, use frozen veggies—they cook just as well. This curry tastes even better the next day, so save some leftovers!

Beef Stroganoff

INGREDIENTS

- 1/2 lb beef strips
- 1 cup mushrooms, sliced
- 1/2 cup sour cream
- 1 cup beef broth
- 1 cup cooked egg noodles

THE BENEFITS

This hearty meal combines lean beef for protein and essential iron with mushrooms rich in antioxidants and fiber. Egg noodles provide energy-boosting carbs, and sour cream offers calcium and a creamy texture. The beef broth enhances hydration and adds depth of flavor without unnecessary calories. This balanced meal satisfies cravings while delivering nutrients to fuel your day.

PREPARATION

- Toss your beef strips with garlic powder, then sear them in a hot skillet for about 2 minutes per side to lock in flavor.
- Slice up the mushrooms and add them to the crockpot along with the beef.
- Pour in the beef broth and give it a stir. Cover and cook on low for 6 hours or high for 3 hours—let the slow cooker do its magic.
- When it's done, stir in the sour cream to create a rich, creamy sauce. Add the cooked egg noodles to the crockpot and gently mix until everything is coated.
- Serve the Stroganoff warm, garnished with fresh parsley for extra flair. Pair with crusty bread for the perfect comfort meal.

RECIPE TIPS

Cook the noodles just before serving to keep them from getting mushy. Sear the beef for added flavor—it makes a difference! Use fresh mushrooms for a firmer texture, but canned work in a pinch. Stir in the sour cream right before serving to keep it creamy and smooth. Leftovers? This dish reheats like a dream—just add a splash of broth to refresh the sauce.

Chicken Taco Filling

INGREDIENTS

- 1/2 lb chicken breasts
- 1/2 cup salsa
- 1 tbsp taco seasoning
- 1/4 cup chicken broth
- 1 tsp lime juice

THE BENEFITS

This Chicken Taco Filling is packed with lean protein from chicken, which supports muscle repair and keeps you full. The salsa and lime juice bring Vitamin C and antioxidants, boosting immunity and adding zesty flavor. Taco seasoning adds minimal calories while packing in taste, and the chicken broth keeps the dish moist without adding unhealthy fats. Simple yet nutritious, this filling is perfect for tacos, bowls, or even salads, offering a flavorful, balanced meal.

PREPARATION

- Place the chicken breasts in the crockpot—don't worry about cutting them, they'll shred later.
- Mix the salsa, taco seasoning, chicken broth, and lime juice in a bowl. Pour this flavorful mixture over the chicken.
- Cover the crockpot and set it to low for 6 hours or high for 3 hours—go about your day while it cooks.
- When the time's up, use two forks to shred the chicken right in the pot. Mix it with the sauce for extra flavor.
- Scoop the filling into warm tortillas, or serve over rice if that's your style. Garnish with cilantro, diced tomatoes, or a squeeze of lime.
- Pair it with sour cream, guac, or your favorite toppings for a complete taco night experience!

RECIPE TIPS

Use fresh lime juice for the best flavor—it makes a huge difference. Don't skip shredding the chicken in the pot; it absorbs all the juicy flavors that way. If you want more heat, throw in a pinch of cayenne or diced jalapeños. Leftovers? Store them for up to 3 days and reheat with a splash of chicken broth. This filling isn't just for tacos—it's amazing in quesadillas, enchiladas, or on top of nachos!

Cheesy Potato Soup

INGREDIENTS

- 1 medium potato (about 8 oz), diced
- 1 cup chicken broth
- 1/2 cup shredded cheddar cheese
- 1/4 cup milk
- 1 slice bacon, cooked and crumbled

THE BENEFITS

Cheesy Potato Soup is packed with comfort and nutrients. Potatoes deliver energy-boosting carbs and potassium, essential for muscle function. Chicken broth is hydrating and loaded with minerals, while cheddar cheese provides calcium and protein. Bacon adds flavor in moderation, and milk contributes additional vitamins and creaminess. This soup strikes the perfect balance of indulgence and wholesome goodness for a cozy, satisfying meal.

PREPARATION

- Dice the potato into small cubes so it cooks faster. Toss it into your crockpot.
- Pour in the chicken broth, making sure it covers the potatoes. Add a pinch of salt if you like.
- Cover the crockpot and cook on low for 6 hours or high for 3 hours until the potatoes are soft.
- Use a potato masher or the back of a spoon to mash some of the potatoes for a creamy texture. Stir in the milk and shredded cheddar cheese until melted and smooth.
- Crumble your cooked bacon and sprinkle it on top as a garnish.
- Ladle the soup into bowls, top with more cheese if you're feeling it, and pair with some crusty bread. Comfort food, sorted.

RECIPE TIPS

Dice the potatoes evenly so they cook at the same rate. For an even creamier soup, blend part of the cooked mixture. Want a smoky kick? Use smoked cheddar or add a dash of paprika. Bacon lovers: cook extra to sprinkle on top! Leftovers reheat beautifully, but add a splash of milk when warming it up to restore the creamy texture. This soup pairs perfectly with a crusty baguette or crackers for dipping.

White Chicken Chili

INGREDIENTS

- 1/2 lb chicken breasts, diced
- 1 cup white beans, cooked
- 1/2 cup chicken broth
- 1/4 cup sour cream
- 1 tsp ground cumin

THE BENEFITS

White Chicken Chili is a protein-packed dish with lean chicken and nutrient-rich white beans that provide fiber and slow-digesting carbs. Cumin adds antioxidants and anti-inflammatory benefits, while chicken broth keeps it light yet flavorful. Sour cream gives a creamy touch without overloading on fats. This dish is hearty and satisfying, making it an excellent choice for balanced nutrition in a comforting, tasty meal.

PREPARATION

- Dice the chicken breasts into small cubes for quick cooking, or leave them whole if you want to shred later. Toss them into your crockpot.
- Add the white beans, chicken broth, and ground cumin. Stir to mix everything evenly.
- Cover the crockpot and cook on low for 6 hours or high for 3 hours. Let the slow cooker work its magic.
- About 15 minutes before it's done, stir in the sour cream to create a creamy, flavorful base. If the chicken is whole, shred it now with two forks.
- Serve the chili hot, topped with fresh cilantro and a slice of lime for some zing. Pair with tortilla chips or cornbread for the perfect meal.

RECIPE TIPS

Want to save time? Use rotisserie chicken and reduce cooking time by half. Mash some beans before stirring them in to thicken the chili. Use fresh lime juice—it adds a bright pop of flavor. Prefer heat? Add a chopped jalapeño or a pinch of chili flakes. If leftovers thicken too much, just add a splash of chicken broth when reheating. Serve with toppings like shredded cheese or avocado for an extra flavor boost.

Vegetarian Lentil Stew

INGREDIENTS

- 1/2 cup lentils, rinsed
- 1 medium carrot, diced (about 4 oz)
- 1/2 cup canned diced tomatoes
- 1 cup vegetable broth
- 1 tsp ground cumin

THE BENEFITS

This Vegetarian Lentil Stew is a powerhouse of plant-based protein, fiber, and essential nutrients. Lentils are packed with iron and folate, while carrots provide Vitamin A for healthy skin and vision. Tomatoes bring antioxidants like lycopene, and vegetable broth keeps it light yet nourishing. With no added fats or processed ingredients, this stew is heart-healthy, filling, and perfect for anyone seeking a nutritious and satisfying meal.

PREPARATION

- Rinse the lentils under cold water and set them aside. Dice the carrot into small cubes—nothing fancy.
- Toss the lentils, carrots, diced tomatoes, and vegetable broth into your crockpot.
- Sprinkle the cumin over the top and give everything a good stir to mix those flavors.
- Cover the crockpot and set it to low for 6 hours or high for 3 hours. Let the lentils soften and soak up all the deliciousness.
- When done, give it a quick stir and serve hot, garnished with fresh parsley or a drizzle of olive oil if you're feeling fancy.
- Pair with crusty bread for dunking, or serve over rice for a hearty meal. Easy, filling, and totally comforting.

RECIPE TIPS

Rinse the lentils well before cooking to remove any debris. Add extra broth if you prefer a thinner stew. Want a smoky twist? Add a pinch of smoked paprika. Dice the carrots evenly to ensure they cook through. If you're short on time, canned lentils can work—just reduce the cooking time. Leftovers? This stew tastes even better the next day as the flavors meld. Serve with a splash of lemon juice for added brightness.

Bacon Cheeseburger Casserole

INGREDIENTS

- 1/2 lb ground beef
- 2 slices bacon, cooked and crumbled
- 1/2 cup shredded cheddar cheese
- 1/2 cup diced tomatoes (canned or fresh)
- 1 tsp garlic powder

THE BENEFITS

Bacon Cheeseburger Casserole offers protein-packed ground beef for muscle repair and satiety, while cheddar cheese adds calcium and healthy fats. Tomatoes bring in Vitamin C and antioxidants, boosting immunity. Bacon, when used in moderation, adds flavor without overloading on calories. With simple, whole ingredients, this dish satisfies comfort food cravings while delivering essential nutrients in a low-carb, hearty meal.

PREPARATION

- Cook the ground beef in a skillet over medium heat until browned, breaking it up as it cooks. Sprinkle in the garlic powder for extra flavor.
- Drain any excess fat from the beef, then transfer it to your crockpot.
- Add the diced tomatoes and mix everything together. Spread it evenly at the bottom of the pot.
- Layer the cooked, crumbled bacon on top of the beef mixture.
- Sprinkle the shredded cheddar cheese over the bacon to create a melty, cheesy topping.
- Cover and cook on low for 2-3 hours, just enough to blend the flavors and melt the cheese.
- Scoop out the casserole and serve it hot. Pair with pickles, toasted buns, or a fresh salad for that classic burger vibe.

RECIPE TIPS

Brown the beef first to lock in flavor—it makes a big difference! Use thick-cut bacon for an extra crispy topping. If you prefer more veggies, add diced onions or bell peppers to the beef mixture. For a creamier texture, mix a tablespoon of cream cheese into the beef before layering. Want some spice? Sprinkle in chili flakes or jalapeños. Leftovers reheat beautifully, making this an ideal meal-prep dish for the week.

Thai Peanut Chicken

INGREDIENTS

- 1/2 lb chicken breasts, cut into strips
- 1/4 cup peanut butter
- 1 tbsp soy sauce
- 1/4 cup coconut milk
- 1 tsp lime juice

THE BENEFITS

Thai Peanut Chicken balances lean protein from chicken with healthy fats from peanut butter and coconut milk. These fats support brain function and keep you full. Lime juice adds Vitamin C, and soy sauce provides umami flavor with minimal added calories. With no processed ingredients, this dish is hearty and nutritious, offering a satisfying mix of protein and healthy energy sources for a well-rounded meal.

PREPARATION

- Slice the chicken into strips and toss it into your crockpot—no need to fuss.
- In a bowl, whisk together the peanut butter, soy sauce, coconut milk, and lime juice until smooth and creamy.
- Pour the sauce over the chicken, making sure it's coated evenly.
- Cover and cook on low for 4-5 hours or high for 2-3 hours. Stir once or twice if you're around to help the flavors blend.
- When done, give it a final stir and serve the chicken over steamed rice or noodles. Garnish with crushed peanuts, fresh cilantro, or an extra squeeze of lime if you want to show off.
- Enjoy the rich, creamy flavors with minimal effort and maximum taste satisfaction.

RECIPE TIPS

Go for natural peanut butter for a purer flavor without added sugars. Use fresh lime juice—it brightens the dish and balances the richness. Stir the sauce a couple of times during cooking to prevent sticking. Want more spice? Add a pinch of red chili flakes or sriracha. Leftovers are fantastic—reheat gently with a splash of coconut milk to revive the creamy sauce. Serve with a side of steamed broccoli or snap peas for extra crunch!

Quinoa and Black Bean Bowl

INGREDIENTS

- 1/2 cup quinoa, rinsed
- 1 cup black beans, cooked
- 1/2 cup diced tomatoes
- 1/4 cup corn kernels
- 1 tsp ground cumin

THE BENEFITS

This Quinoa and Black Bean Bowl is a nutrient-packed, plant-based meal. Quinoa is a complete protein, providing all essential amino acids, while black beans add fiber and iron. Corn and tomatoes deliver antioxidants like Vitamin C and beta-carotene, promoting healthy skin and immunity. Ground cumin enhances flavor without extra calories, and the dish is naturally gluten-free. This balanced, colorful bowl offers long-lasting energy and vital nutrients, making it a guilt-free comfort meal.

PREPARATION

- Rinse the quinoa thoroughly and toss it into your crockpot. Add 1 cup of water for cooking.
- Stir in the black beans, diced tomatoes, corn, and ground cumin. Mix everything well to spread the flavors evenly.
- Cover and set the crockpot to low for 4 hours or high for 2 hours. Let the quinoa absorb all the delicious juices.
- Once the quinoa is tender and fluffy, give everything a final stir to ensure it's perfectly mixed.
- Serve in bowls, topped with fresh cilantro, a squeeze of lime, or a dollop of salsa for extra flair.
- Pair with tortilla chips or enjoy it as a standalone meal—it's hearty, filling, and bursting with flavor!

RECIPE TIPS

Rinse the quinoa thoroughly to remove its natural bitterness. For added spice, toss in a pinch of chili powder or smoked paprika. Prefer more crunch? Top with sliced avocado or chopped bell peppers. Stir occasionally if you're around to prevent sticking. Use fresh lime juice to brighten up the flavors right before serving. Got leftovers? This dish is great cold—just toss it in a salad or wrap it in a tortilla for a quick next-day meal.

Stuffed Bell Peppers

INGREDIENTS

- 2 medium bell peppers
- 1/2 cup cooked rice
- 1/2 cup ground beef, cooked
- 1/4 cup diced tomatoes
- 1/4 cup shredded cheddar cheese

THE BENEFITS

Stuffed Bell Peppers combine protein, fiber, and essential vitamins in one delicious package. Bell peppers are loaded with Vitamin C and antioxidants, supporting immune health. Ground beef provides iron and protein for energy, while rice adds slow-digesting carbs for sustained energy. Tomatoes bring in lycopene, promoting heart health, and cheese offers calcium and a touch of healthy fat. This balanced, nutrient-rich dish is filling, flavorful, and perfect for a hearty, wholesome meal.

PREPARATION

- Cut the tops off the bell peppers and scoop out the seeds—get them ready for the filling.
- In a bowl, mix the cooked rice, cooked ground beef, and diced tomatoes until it's a well-blended filling. Add a pinch of salt and pepper for extra flavor.
- Stuff the bell peppers generously with the filling and place them upright in your crockpot.
- Cover and cook on low for 4 hours or high for 2 hours, letting the peppers soften and the flavors meld.
- About 15 minutes before serving, sprinkle shredded cheddar cheese on top of each pepper. Cover again and cook until the cheese melts.
- Serve the peppers hot, garnished with parsley or a dollop of sour cream. Pair with a fresh salad or some crusty bread for a complete meal.

RECIPE TIPS

Choose firm bell peppers so they hold their shape during cooking. Pre-cook the ground beef to save time and ensure even seasoning. If you like a little kick, mix in red chili flakes or diced jalapeños. Use parchment paper in the crockpot to prevent sticking. For extra creaminess, add a spoonful of sour cream to the filling. Got leftovers? Chop them up and toss them in a salad or wrap them in a tortilla for a quick next-day meal!

Garlic Mashed Potatoes

INGREDIENTS

- 2 medium potatoes (about 12 oz), peeled and cubed
- 1/4 cup milk
- 1 tbsp butter
- 1 tsp garlic powder
- 1/2 tsp salt

THE BENEFITS

Garlic Mashed Potatoes are a simple, nutrient-packed side dish. Potatoes provide potassium for muscle health and energy-boosting carbs. Garlic powder adds a touch of flavor while delivering heart-health benefits. Milk and butter contribute calcium and healthy fats, ensuring a smooth, creamy texture. This recipe is low in processed ingredients and serves as a comforting yet nutritious accompaniment to any meal, providing vitamins and minerals in every bite.

PREPARATION

- Peel and cube the potatoes, then toss them into your crockpot. Add just enough water to cover them.
- Sprinkle in the garlic powder and salt to start building the flavor.
- Cover the crockpot and set it to high for 3-4 hours, or low for 6-7 hours, until the potatoes are fork-tender.
- Drain the water and mash the potatoes right in the crockpot using a masher or a sturdy fork.
- Stir in the milk and butter, letting the heat melt the butter into creamy goodness. Mix until the texture is smooth.
- Scoop the mashed potatoes into a serving dish, garnish with chives or a pat of butter, and enjoy alongside your favorite main dish!

RECIPE TIPS

Cut the potatoes into even pieces for consistent cooking. If you prefer a stronger garlic flavor, add a clove of roasted garlic instead of garlic powder. Use warm milk to avoid cooling down the mashed potatoes. For a richer taste, swap regular butter with salted or herb-infused butter. Leftovers? Turn them into potato cakes by frying them lightly the next day. Mashed potatoes are versatile, so don't hesitate to mix in cheese, chives, or even a dollop of sour cream!

Honey-Glazed Carrots

INGREDIENTS

- 1/2 lb baby carrots
- 2 tbsp honey
- 1 tbsp butter
- 1/2 tsp garlic powder
- 1/4 tsp salt

THE BENEFITS

Honey-Glazed Carrots are a simple yet nutrient-rich side dish. Carrots are packed with Vitamin A for healthy vision and antioxidants to boost immunity. Honey provides natural sweetness and energy, while butter adds a touch of healthy fat for flavor and satisfaction. Garlic powder enhances the taste with minimal calories, and the dish is low in processed ingredients. This combination delivers a healthy dose of vitamins and minerals while satisfying your craving for a sweet and savory treat.

PREPARATION

- Toss the baby carrots into your crockpot and sprinkle them with garlic powder and salt to start the flavor party.
- Melt the butter in the microwave and mix it with the honey until it's smooth and golden. Pour this sweet mixture over the carrots, making sure they're well coated.
- Cover the crockpot and cook on low for 4 hours or high for 2 hours, letting the carrots soak in that honey goodness. Stir once or twice if you're around.
- When they're tender and shiny, scoop them out into a serving dish. Drizzle any leftover glaze from the pot over the top.
- Garnish with fresh parsley or a sprinkle of black pepper if you're feeling fancy. Serve warm as a sweet and savory side dish.

RECIPE TIPS

Use fresh baby carrots for the best flavor and texture. If you don't have baby carrots, cut regular carrots into even slices. Stir occasionally to ensure the glaze coats the carrots evenly. Want an extra kick? Add a pinch of cinnamon or cayenne to the honey mix. Leftovers reheat beautifully—just warm them in the microwave or a skillet. This dish pairs perfectly with roasted chicken or grilled fish for a balanced, colorful plate!

Mexican Rice

INGREDIENTS

- 1/2 cup long-grain white rice
- 1/4 cup diced tomatoes
- 1/4 cup chicken broth
- 1/2 tsp cumin
- 1/4 cup chopped onion

THE BENEFITS

Mexican Rice is a flavorful and nutritious side dish. Rice provides complex carbs for sustained energy, while tomatoes and onions are packed with antioxidants and vitamins. Chicken broth adds essential minerals without extra fat, and cumin brings anti-inflammatory benefits. This simple recipe is low in fat and rich in wholesome ingredients, making it a versatile addition to any meal while delivering flavor and nutritional value in every bite.

PREPARATION

- Rinse the rice under cold water to remove excess starch, then toss it into your crockpot.
- Add the diced tomatoes, chicken broth, chopped onion, and sprinkle in the cumin. Stir everything together to combine the flavors.
- Cover the crockpot and cook on low for 2-3 hours or high for 1-1.5 hours. Give it a stir halfway through to make sure the rice cooks evenly.
- Once the rice is tender and fluffy, give it a final stir to mix in all the flavors.
- Scoop it into bowls and garnish with fresh cilantro, a wedge of lime, or a sprinkle of cheese for extra flair. Pair with tacos, grilled chicken, or beans for a full meal.

RECIPE TIPS

Rinse the rice well to keep it from getting sticky. Stir halfway through cooking to avoid clumps. Use vegetable broth for a vegetarian version, or add a pinch of chili powder for a spicier kick. Prefer a smoky flavor? Toss in a bit of smoked paprika. Leftovers heat up perfectly in the microwave—just sprinkle with a little water before reheating to keep it moist. Serve alongside enchiladas or grilled fish for a complete, crowd-pleasing dinner!

Green Bean Casserole

INGREDIENTS

- 1/2 lb fresh green beans, trimmed
- 1/4 cup cream of mushroom soup
- 1/4 cup milk
- 1/4 cup crispy fried onions
- 1/4 tsp garlic powder

THE BENEFITS

Green Bean Casserole combines the fiber and vitamins of fresh green beans with the rich flavor of cream of mushroom soup. Green beans are loaded with antioxidants and Vitamin K, supporting bone health and immunity. Garlic powder adds a touch of heart-healthy flavor, and crispy onions bring texture without overwhelming calories. This dish is satisfying and wholesome, providing a perfect balance of indulgence and nutrition, making it a great choice for family dinners.

PREPARATION

- Wash and trim the green beans, then toss them into your crockpot. Keep them whole or cut them in half —your call.
- In a small bowl, mix the cream of mushroom soup, milk, and garlic powder. Pour this creamy goodness over the green beans, ensuring they're coated.
- Cover and cook on low for 4 hours or high for 2 hours, letting the beans get tender and the flavors meld together.
- About 15 minutes before serving, sprinkle the crispy fried onions on top. Cover again just long enough for them to warm up.
- Serve hot, garnished with a sprinkle of fresh parsley or extra crispy onions for crunch. Pair with roasted chicken or turkey for the ultimate comfort meal.

RECIPE TIPS

Use fresh green beans for the best crunch, but frozen ones work in a pinch—just thaw before cooking. Want more flavor? Add a pinch of smoked paprika or a splash of Worcestershire sauce to the creamy mixture. Stir the casserole gently before topping with onions to ensure every bite is coated in sauce. Don't overcook; you want the beans tender, not mushy. Leftovers reheat well in the oven for a crispier topping.

Crispy Brussels Sprouts

INGREDIENTS

- 1/2 lb Brussels sprouts, halved
- 1 tbsp olive oil
- 1 tsp garlic powder
- 1/4 tsp sea salt
- 1 tbsp grated Parmesan cheese

THE BENEFITS

Crispy Brussels Sprouts are a nutrient-dense powerhouse. Loaded with Vitamin C and K, they support immune health and strong bones. Olive oil provides heart-healthy fats, while garlic powder adds antioxidants without extra calories. Parmesan cheese offers a touch of calcium and umami flavor. This dish is low in carbs, high in fiber, and delivers essential vitamins and minerals for a guilt-free, delicious side or snack.

PREPARATION

- Wash and halve the Brussels sprouts, tossing them into your crockpot for an easy setup.
- Drizzle olive oil over the sprouts, making sure they're lightly coated. Sprinkle on the garlic powder and sea salt, then toss everything to mix well.
- Cover and cook on high for 2-3 hours or low for 4-5 hours, letting the sprouts soften and take on some serious flavor.
- About 15 minutes before serving, sprinkle Parmesan cheese over the top, leaving the lid slightly open for extra crispness.
- Serve these golden-brown beauties hot, garnished with fresh parsley or a squeeze of lemon for added zest. Pair them with roasted chicken or fish, or enjoy them as a snack.

RECIPE TIPS

For even crispier results, leave the lid slightly ajar during the last 30 minutes of cooking. Fresh Parmesan works best—grate it just before sprinkling. If you like a smoky kick, toss in a pinch of smoked paprika or chili flakes. Use fresh garlic instead of powder for a more robust flavor. Leftovers? Reheat them in the oven to revive the crispiness. Pair with a garlic aioli or honey-mustard dip for next-level flavor!

Cheesy Spinach Dip

INGREDIENTS

- 2 cups fresh spinach, chopped
- 1/2 cup cream cheese, softened
- 1/4 cup sour cream
- 1/4 cup shredded mozzarella cheese
- 1 tsp garlic powder

THE BENEFITS

Cheesy Spinach Dip delivers a mix of flavor and nutrients. Spinach is a superfood packed with iron, calcium, and Vitamin K, supporting bone health and immunity. Cream cheese and sour cream add protein and a touch of healthy fat, while mozzarella contributes calcium and cheesy satisfaction. With its nutrient-dense spinach base and creamy textures, this dip makes an indulgent but nutritious appetizer or snack.

PREPARATION

- Chop the fresh spinach and toss it into your crockpot. Spread it out evenly for a good base.
- Add the softened cream cheese, sour cream, and garlic powder on top of the spinach. Don't stir just yet—let the heat do its thing.
- Cover and cook on low for 2 hours or high for 1 hour. Stir occasionally to ensure everything melts and blends together.
- About 15 minutes before serving, sprinkle the shredded mozzarella on top and let it melt into a gooey layer of cheesy goodness.
- Serve the dip hot with tortilla chips, crackers, or sliced baguette. Garnish with fresh parsley for extra flair, and enjoy the creamy, cheesy masterpiece.

RECIPE TIPS

Use fresh spinach for the best flavor and texture, but frozen works too—just thaw and drain it first. Stir occasionally for a smoother blend. Want more kick? Add a pinch of red pepper flakes or chopped jalapeños. Use a broiler for 2 minutes after cooking to get a golden crust on the cheese. Leftovers? Reheat gently in the microwave or oven, and serve with fresh chips or veggies. Perfect for game nights or parties!

Nacho Cheese Sauce

INGREDIENTS

- 1/2 cup shredded cheddar cheese
- 1/4 cup milk
- 1 tsp butter
- 1/2 tsp cornstarch
- 1/4 tsp smoked paprika

THE BENEFITS

This Nacho Cheese Sauce is simple, flavorful, and satisfying. Cheese provides calcium and protein, supporting strong bones and muscles. Milk adds extra calcium and creaminess, while paprika brings antioxidants with a subtle smoky taste. Butter offers a small amount of healthy fats, and cornstarch thickens the sauce without extra calories. This recipe is a delicious way to add nutrients to your favorite snacks without relying on heavily processed store-bought dips.

PREPARATION

- Toss the shredded cheddar cheese, milk, butter, and cornstarch into your crockpot. No need to stir just yet—let the heat take care of it.
- Cover the crockpot and cook on low for 1 hour. Give it a quick stir every 20 minutes to help the cheese melt evenly.
- Once everything is melted and smooth, sprinkle in the smoked paprika for that extra kick of flavor. Stir it one last time to mix the spices evenly.
- Serve the nacho cheese sauce hot, garnished with fresh cilantro if you're feeling fancy. Pair it with tortilla chips, veggie sticks, or even drizzle it over fries.
- This creamy, cheesy dip is guaranteed to upgrade your snack game. Enjoy it while it's warm and gooey!

RECIPE TIPS

Use freshly shredded cheese for the best melt—it blends smoother than pre-packaged shredded cheese. Stir occasionally to avoid lumps and keep the sauce velvety. Add a pinch of chili powder or jalapeños if you like it spicy. Leftovers can be reheated gently with a splash of milk to revive the creamy texture. Pair the sauce with nachos, soft pretzels, or use it as a topping for burgers. This dip is versatile and sure to please!

Creamy Corn Casserole

INGREDIENTS

- 1 cup canned corn, drained
- 1/4 cup sour cream
- 1/4 cup shredded cheddar cheese
- 1/4 cup cornmeal
- 1 tbsp butter, melted

THE BENEFITS

Creamy Corn Casserole is a comforting dish packed with fiber and essential vitamins. Corn provides a healthy dose of Vitamin C, antioxidants, and natural sweetness. Sour cream adds calcium and a creamy texture, while cheddar cheese delivers protein and flavor. Cornmeal contributes whole grains, promoting good digestion and long-lasting energy. This dish is a perfect blend of hearty and healthy, making it a crowd-pleasing side or a cozy main course.

PREPARATION

- Drain the canned corn and toss it into your crockpot. Spread it out evenly to form the base.
- In a bowl, mix the sour cream, shredded cheddar cheese, and melted butter. Stir in the cornmeal to create a thick, creamy mixture.
- Pour the mixture over the corn in the crockpot, spreading it out with a spoon so everything's covered.
- Cover and cook on low for 3-4 hours or high for 1.5-2 hours until the casserole is set and slightly golden around the edges.
- Scoop the casserole into bowls, garnish with fresh parsley if desired, and serve hot. Pair it with grilled chicken or a fresh salad for a complete meal. Enjoy the creamy, cheesy goodness!

RECIPE TIPS

Use fresh corn if it's in season for an even sweeter flavor. Stir halfway through cooking for even consistency. Add a pinch of chili powder or smoked paprika for a smoky kick. To make it extra cheesy, sprinkle a little more cheddar on top during the last 15 minutes. Leftovers reheat wonderfully in the oven—just cover with foil to retain moisture. Serve it with a dollop of sour cream or a drizzle of honey for added flair.

Red Wine Braised Short Ribs

INGREDIENTS

- 1 lb beef short ribs
- 1 cup red wine
- 1/2 cup beef broth
- 1 medium onion, sliced (about 4 oz)
- 1 tsp garlic powder

THE BENEFITS

Red Wine Braised Short Ribs are packed with flavor and nutrients. Beef short ribs provide protein, iron, and essential amino acids, while red wine offers antioxidants that support heart health. Onions add Vitamin C and natural sweetness, and beef broth contributes hydration and minerals. This dish is a luxurious comfort meal with balanced macronutrients, making it a satisfying choice for special occasions or indulgent dinners.

PREPARATION

- Season the short ribs with salt and pepper, then sear them in a hot skillet for 2-3 minutes per side until browned.
- Place the short ribs in your crockpot and top with sliced onion.
- Mix the red wine, beef broth, and garlic powder in a small bowl. Pour this mixture over the ribs, making sure they're well coated.
- Cover and cook on low for 8 hours or high for 4-5 hours. The ribs should be tender and falling off the bone.
- Serve the short ribs hot with the rich sauce spooned over the top. Pair with mashed potatoes, roasted vegetables, or crusty bread for a hearty meal. Garnish with fresh rosemary or parsley for a touch of elegance.

RECIPE TIPS

Sear the ribs before slow cooking to lock in flavor. Use a dry red wine like Cabernet Sauvignon for the richest sauce. Stir occasionally to make sure the sauce doesn't stick. For extra thickness, whisk a teaspoon of cornstarch with water and stir it into the sauce 30 minutes before serving. Leftovers taste even better the next day—serve over pasta or rice for a quick, hearty meal. Enjoy the melt-in-your-mouth tenderness!

Chicken Marsala

INGREDIENTS

- 2 chicken breasts (about 1 lb)
- 1 cup sliced mushrooms
- 1/2 cup Marsala wine
- 1/4 cup chicken broth
- 1 tbsp butter

THE BENEFITS

Chicken Marsala is a balanced, flavorful dish. Chicken provides lean protein essential for muscle repair, while mushrooms offer antioxidants and fiber. Marsala wine adds depth without excessive calories, and chicken broth enriches the dish with minerals. The butter contributes a creamy texture and healthy fats in moderation. This meal is hearty, nourishing, and perfect for a satisfying dinner.

PREPARATION

- Pound the chicken breasts to an even thickness and season with salt and pepper on both sides.
- Heat butter in a skillet, then sear the chicken for about 2-3 minutes per side until golden. Transfer to your crockpot.
- In the same skillet, sauté the mushrooms until tender. Add them to the crockpot over the chicken.
- Pour Marsala wine and chicken broth into the crockpot, ensuring the chicken and mushrooms are coated in the sauce.
- Cover and cook on low for 4-5 hours or high for 2-3 hours until the chicken is tender.
- Serve hot, topped with the rich sauce and mushrooms. Pair with mashed potatoes or pasta, and garnish with fresh parsley for an elegant touch.

RECIPE TIPS

Pound the chicken for even cooking and a tender texture. Sear it first to lock in the juices and boost flavor. Use dry Marsala wine for the best sauce consistency. Want more richness? Add a splash of cream to the sauce before serving. Stir occasionally if you're around to keep the flavors melded. Leftovers? Reheat gently to keep the chicken moist and the sauce intact. Pair with crusty bread to soak up every last drop!

Lemon Butter Salmon

INGREDIENTS

- 2 salmon fillets (about 8 oz each)
- 2 tbsp butter, melted
- 1 tbsp fresh lemon juice
- 1/2 tsp garlic powder
- 1/4 tsp salt

THE BENEFITS

Lemon Butter Salmon is packed with omega-3 fatty acids, essential for heart and brain health. Salmon is also a great source of lean protein and Vitamin D. The fresh lemon juice boosts Vitamin C, enhancing immunity, while butter adds healthy fats in moderation for flavor and satiety. Garlic powder provides antioxidants, rounding out this nutrient-rich dish that's indulgent yet perfectly balanced for a healthy lifestyle.

PREPARATION

- Place the salmon fillets skin-side down in your crockpot—no need to overthink it.
- Mix the melted butter, fresh lemon juice, garlic powder, and salt in a small bowl. Drizzle this buttery goodness evenly over the fillets.
- Cover and cook on low for 1.5-2 hours. The salmon is done when it flakes easily with a fork and is tender but not overcooked.
- Carefully lift the fillets out of the crockpot and plate them up. Spoon some of the leftover sauce from the pot over the top for extra flavor.
- Serve hot, garnished with fresh dill or lemon slices if you want to impress. Pair it with asparagus, rice, or a simple salad for a quick and fancy meal.

RECIPE TIPS

Don't overcook the salmon—check for flakiness after 1.5 hours. For extra flavor, sprinkle a pinch of dill or parsley before serving. Want a crispy edge? Sear the fillets for 1-2 minutes in a hot pan after slow cooking. Add a splash of white wine to the butter mixture for a more sophisticated sauce. Leftovers? Reheat gently in the microwave or enjoy cold in a salad the next day. Serve with roasted veggies for a complete, healthy plate!

Shrimp Scampi Pasta

INGREDIENTS

- 1/2 lb shrimp, peeled and deveined
- 4 oz spaghetti or linguine
- 2 tbsp butter
- 1 tbsp olive oil
- 1 tsp minced garlic

THE BENEFITS

Shrimp Scampi Pasta is a protein-packed dish that's light yet satisfying. Shrimp provides lean protein and omega-3 fatty acids for heart health, while garlic adds antioxidants. Butter and olive oil deliver healthy fats for energy and flavor. Pasta supplies carbs for sustained energy, making it a balanced meal. This dish is indulgent yet nutritious, perfect for a quick, wholesome dinner.

PREPARATION

- Cook the pasta according to the package instructions, drain it, and set aside.
- Heat butter and olive oil in your crockpot on the sauté setting (or use a pan if your crockpot lacks this feature). Add the minced garlic and let it sizzle for a minute.
- Toss the shrimp into the crockpot and cook until pink, about 2-3 minutes per side.
- Add the cooked pasta to the crockpot and toss everything to coat in the buttery garlic sauce. Cook on low for 30 minutes to let the flavors meld.
- Serve hot, garnished with fresh parsley and a squeeze of lemon. Pair with garlic bread for the ultimate comfort meal.

RECIPE TIPS

Don't overcook the shrimp—it gets rubbery. Use fresh garlic for the best flavor and aroma. Prefer a zesty twist? Add red pepper flakes or a splash of white wine to the sauce. Toss the pasta well to ensure every strand is coated in buttery goodness. Want more richness? Sprinkle grated Parmesan cheese before serving. Leftovers? Reheat gently with a splash of olive oil to revive the sauce. Enjoy it with a glass of chilled white wine!

Garlic Butter Steak Bites

INGREDIENTS

- 1/2 lb sirloin steak, cubed
- 2 tbsp butter
- 1 tsp minced garlic
- 1/4 tsp salt
- 1 tbsp chopped parsley

THE BENEFITS

Garlic Butter Steak Bites are a protein-packed, low-carb option. Sirloin steak provides essential amino acids and iron for energy and muscle repair. Butter adds healthy fats, and garlic delivers antioxidants with anti-inflammatory benefits. Parsley contributes a dose of Vitamin C and freshness to the dish. This recipe is indulgent yet balanced, offering high-quality nutrients and a satisfying flavor that fits into various dietary plans.

PREPARATION

- Cube the sirloin steak into bite-sized pieces and season with salt.
- Heat butter in your crockpot on the sauté setting, or use a skillet if your crockpot lacks this feature. Add the garlic and let it sizzle for about 30 seconds.
- Toss in the steak bites and sear for 2-3 minutes until browned on all sides. Stir occasionally to coat the steak in garlic butter.
- Cover and slow cook on low for 1.5-2 hours, allowing the flavors to meld.
- Before serving, sprinkle chopped parsley over the top for a fresh touch.
- Serve hot with a side of mashed potatoes, steamed veggies, or crusty bread to soak up the buttery sauce. Enjoy the ultimate steak experience!

RECIPE TIPS

For extra tenderness, let the steak come to room temperature before cooking. Don't overcrowd the pot; cook in batches if necessary for even searing. Use fresh garlic for the best aroma and flavor. Like a little heat? Add a pinch of chili flakes. Pair with roasted veggies or toss over rice for a filling meal. Leftovers make great steak sandwiches or wraps—just reheat gently to keep them juicy!

Stuffed Portobello Mushrooms

INGREDIENTS

- 2 large portobello mushrooms
- 1/4 cup breadcrumbs
- 1/4 cup shredded mozzarella cheese
- 1 tbsp olive oil
- 1 tsp minced garlic

THE BENEFITS

Stuffed Portobello Mushrooms are a healthy, flavorful choice. Portobellos are low in calories and rich in antioxidants, potassium, and Vitamin D, supporting bone health and immunity. Breadcrumbs and cheese provide satisfying carbs and protein, while garlic adds antioxidants. Olive oil offers heart-healthy fats. This dish is a nutrient-dense way to enjoy a light yet filling meal packed with natural goodness and indulgent flavors.

PREPARATION

- Remove the stems from the portobello mushrooms and brush the caps with olive oil, inside and out. Place them in your crockpot, gill side up.
- In a small bowl, mix the breadcrumbs, shredded mozzarella, and minced garlic. Add a pinch of salt and pepper to season.
- Spoon the breadcrumb mixture into the mushroom caps, packing it gently but not too tightly.
- Cover and cook on low for 2-3 hours, or until the mushrooms are tender and the topping is golden and bubbly.
- Carefully remove the mushrooms and plate them. Garnish with fresh parsley or a sprinkle of Parmesan cheese for extra flair.
- Serve hot as a light meal or pair with a salad or roasted vegetables for a complete dinner.

RECIPE TIPS

Choose firm mushrooms for the best results—they hold their shape better during cooking. Don't skimp on olive oil; it keeps the mushrooms juicy. For added crunch, broil the mushrooms for 2 minutes after slow cooking. Use fresh garlic for a bold flavor, or toss in some chopped herbs for extra zest. Leftovers? Reheat in the oven to keep the topping crispy. These are great as a snack, side, or even a meatless main dish!

Honey Glazed Ham

INGREDIENTS

- 1 lb precooked ham
- 2 tbsp honey
- 1 tbsp Dijon mustard
- 1 tbsp brown sugar
- 1/4 tsp ground cloves
- 1/2 cup pineapple chunks (optional garnish)
- 1/2 orange, sliced (optional garnish)

THE BENEFITS

Honey Glazed Ham is packed with protein and natural sweetness that fuels your energy and satisfies your hunger. The honey adds antioxidants while the tangy glaze brings a bold kick of flavor. Cloves are the secret weapon here, giving a rich spice boost while keeping it hearty. It's simple, filling, and just the right balance of bold and satisfying—a meal that's tough to beat.

PREPARATION

- Fire up the crockpot on low and grease it a bit— don't skip this unless you like cleaning up a sticky mess later.
- Drop the ham in, making sure it fits nice and snug. No wrestling matches with the lid!
- Mix up honey, Dijon mustard, brown sugar, and cloves in a bowl. This is your flavor bomb.
- Pour the glaze all over the ham. Don't be shy—make sure it's covered.
- Cover it up and let it cook for 3–4 hours. Baste it with the juices every hour for max flavor.
- Toss in the pineapple chunks and orange slices for the last hour. Let them soak up all the goodness.
- Pull that beauty out, slap it on a plate, and garnish with the fruits. Dig in like a champion.

RECIPE TIPS

To nail this dish, don't skip basting—it makes the ham juicy and flavorful. Go big with a sticky glaze by cranking the crockpot to high for the last 20 minutes. The pineapple and orange aren't just for show; they add a bold pop of freshness. Pair it with roasted potatoes or a cold beer, and you've got a meal fit for kings.

Spaghetti Carbonara

INGREDIENTS

- 6 oz spaghetti
- 3 oz pancetta or bacon, diced
- 2 large egg yolks
- 1/4 cup grated Parmesan cheese
- 1/4 tsp freshly ground black pepper

THE BENEFITS

Spaghetti Carbonara is a powerhouse meal. The eggs and cheese deliver protein and calcium, while the pancetta adds a satisfying dose of flavor and fats. Combined with the energy-packed carbs in the spaghetti, it's a meal that keeps you going without making you feel weighed down. Comfort food that hits all the right spots.

PREPARATION

- Boil spaghetti in salted water until al dente. Save 1/2 cup pasta water. Drain the rest.
- Fry pancetta in a skillet until crispy—don't drain the fat; it's liquid gold.
- Beat egg yolks with Parmesan and black pepper in a bowl.
- Toss hot pasta in the skillet with pancetta, removing it from the heat. Add egg mixture, stirring fast to create a creamy sauce.
- Loosen with a splash of pasta water if needed. No heat, no scrambled eggs!
- Plate up, hit it with extra cheese and pepper, and devour.

RECIPE TIPS

Keep it smooth by working fast when adding the egg mix—heat is your enemy here. Use that starchy pasta water to fine-tune the sauce's creaminess. Always go big on fresh-ground black pepper for that signature kick. A crisp beer or dry white wine? Perfect partners for this classic dude-approved dinner.

Chocolate Lava Cake

INGREDIENTS

- 4 oz dark chocolate
- 1/4 cup unsalted butter
- 1/4 cup granulated sugar
- 2 large eggs
- 2 tbsp all-purpose flour
- Raspberries of Mint (optional)

THE BENEFITS

This dessert is about quality indulgence. Dark chocolate is rich in antioxidants and can improve heart health and mood. Eggs provide protein, while a small amount of butter and sugar keeps it rich without going overboard. By making it at home, you control the portions and ingredients, enjoying a treat that's indulgent yet thoughtful.

PREPARATION

- Melt chocolate and butter together until smooth. Let it cool slightly.
- Whisk eggs and sugar until pale and fluffy, then fold in the melted chocolate mixture.
- Gently mix in the flour until just combined—don't overdo it.
- Grease two small ramekins, pour in the batter, and cover loosely with foil.
- Pop them into a crockpot with a bit of water at the bottom to steam. Cook on high for 30 minutes or until set outside but molten inside.
- Serve warm, dusted with powdered sugar, with a dollop of whipped cream or some fresh berries on the side.

RECIPE TIPS

Keep it simple—use quality dark chocolate for the best flavor. Test the cakes by touching the tops; they should be set but jiggle a little in the middle. Don't overcook—this is all about that gooey center. Serve it hot and pair it with a shot of espresso or a scoop of vanilla ice cream for next-level indulgence. This is the kind of dessert that's easy to make but looks like you went all out.

Apple Crisp

INGREDIENTS

- 2 medium apples, peeled and sliced
- 2 tbsp brown sugar
- 1/4 cup rolled oats
- 2 tbsp butter, melted
- 1/2 tsp ground cinnamon
- 2 scoops vanilla ice cream (optional garnish)

THE BENEFITS

Apple Crisp combines wholesome apples rich in fiber and vitamin C with heart-healthy oats. Cinnamon adds flavor and a boost of antioxidants, while brown sugar and butter are kept in moderation for just the right sweetness. It's a dessert that satisfies your cravings without going overboard on calories —classic comfort food done right.

PREPARATION

- Slice the apples and toss them with a bit of cinnamon and a pinch of brown sugar—set them aside.
- In a bowl, mix oats, melted butter, and the remaining brown sugar. That's your golden topping.
- Layer the apples in the bottom of your crockpot. Cover them with the oat mixture.
- Cover and cook on high for 2–3 hours or until the apples are soft and the topping is golden.
- Serve it hot with a scoop of vanilla ice cream or a drizzle of cream. This one's a game-changer.

RECIPE TIPS

Keep the apples consistent—thin slices cook evenly. For the topping, don't skimp on butter—it's what makes it crisp. Want an upgrade? Toss a handful of nuts into the oat mix for extra crunch. Serve it straight out of the crockpot with vanilla ice cream for the ultimate comfort food experience. A great dessert that's easy, rustic, and guaranteed to impress.

Peach Cobbler

INGREDIENTS

- 2 medium peaches, sliced
- 1/4 cup granulated sugar
- 1/4 cup self-rising flour
- 2 tbsp butter, melted
- 1/4 tsp ground cinnamon

THE BENEFITS

Peach Cobbler celebrates the natural sweetness of peaches, a fruit loaded with vitamins A and C and fiber. Cinnamon not only enhances flavor but also provides antioxidants. By making this dessert at home, you control the sugar and fat content, keeping it satisfying without going overboard. A warm, fruit-filled dessert that feels indulgent but nourishes, too.

PREPARATION

- Slice the peaches and toss them with sugar and cinnamon in a bowl. This is where the flavor magic starts.
- Pour the peaches into a greased crockpot. No need to overthink it—just get them in there.
- Mix the flour and melted butter into a thick batter. Spread it over the peaches—don't worry if it's not perfect.
- Cover and cook on high for 2–3 hours, or until the topping is golden and the peaches are bubbling.
- Scoop it onto plates, slap on a dollop of vanilla ice cream, and dig in like a champ.

RECIPE TIPS

Make sure those peaches are ripe for max sweetness—no hard ones allowed. Keep the batter thick; it'll bake into a fluffy, golden topping. Want a little extra crunch? Add a sprinkle of sugar on the batter before cooking. For bonus points, serve it hot with a scoop of vanilla ice cream. Nothing says "winning" like warm peaches and cold ice cream on the same plate.

Brownies

INGREDIENTS

- 1/2 cup all-purpose flour
- 1/4 cup cocoa powder
- 1/2 cup granulated sugar
- 1/4 cup melted butter
- 1 large egg

THE BENEFITS

These brownies are simple, with just a few wholesome ingredients. Eggs bring protein, while cocoa powder is packed with antioxidants. The butter adds richness and energy without going overboard. By making them in a slow cooker, you control the portion sizes and sweetness, keeping this treat indulgent yet manageable. Perfect for satisfying cravings the smart way.

PREPARATION

- Whisk the egg and sugar together in a bowl until smooth. You're building the base for the gooey goodness.
- Stir in the melted butter and cocoa powder, mixing until it looks rich and chocolatey.
- Add the flour bit by bit, combining until you've got a thick batter.
- Grease your crockpot and pour in the batter. Smooth the top—it doesn't have to be perfect.
- Cover and cook on high for 2 hours or until the edges are firm but the center is soft.
- Let it cool a bit, then slice it up and enjoy the fudgy glory.

RECIPE TIPS

Don't overmix the batter—keep it just combined for that perfect texture. Grease the crockpot well; you don't want to lose a crumb. Check the brownies early; slow cookers can vary. If you like a gooier center, pull them out sooner. Add a sprinkle of chocolate chips or nuts to the batter for extra punch. Serve warm with a cold glass of milk—it's the ultimate comfort dessert.

Rice Pudding

INGREDIENTS

- 1/2 cup uncooked rice
- 1 cup whole milk
- 1/4 cup granulated sugar
- 1/4 tsp vanilla extract
- 1/4 tsp ground cinnamon
- 2 tbsp raisins (optional garnish)
- Fresh mint leaves (optional garnish)

THE BENEFITS

This Rice Pudding is as comforting as it gets while staying simple and wholesome. Rice provides energy-packed carbs, milk adds calcium and protein, and a touch of cinnamon brings antioxidants and flavor. With just a handful of pantry staples, this dessert is indulgent without being over the top—a perfect balance of cozy and nutritious.

PREPARATION

- Rinse the rice under cold water and toss it into your crockpot. No shortcuts here—it's key for the perfect texture.
- Add milk, sugar, and vanilla extract. Give it a good stir to mix everything up.
- Cover and cook on low for 2–3 hours, stirring occasionally to keep it from sticking.
- Once the rice is tender and the pudding's creamy, it's ready to roll. Sprinkle with cinnamon and give it a taste.
- Serve it warm or chill it if that's your vibe. Either way, it's a winner.

RECIPE TIPS

Keep an eye on the crockpot—it's easy to overcook rice. Stir every now and then to prevent sticking or clumps. Want a richer texture? Swap some milk for cream. Love extras? Toss in raisins or a pat of butter for added depth. Serve it up with a little more cinnamon dusted on top—it's a simple move that makes it pop. Warm, creamy, and made for easy chilling if you're planning ahead.

Banana Bread Pudding

INGREDIENTS

- 2 cups cubed bread (preferably day-old)
- 1 large ripe banana, sliced
- 1/2 cup whole milk
- 1/4 cup granulated sugar
- 1/2 tsp vanilla extract
- Banana and min (optional)

THE BENEFITS

Banana Bread Pudding delivers comfort with a nutritional punch. Bananas bring potassium and natural sweetness, while milk adds calcium and protein. Using day-old bread minimizes food waste and gives you a hearty dessert. The ingredients are simple and wholesome, making this a satisfying, guilt-free treat to enjoy any day of the week.

PREPARATION

- Toss the bread cubes and banana slices into your crockpot. Arrange them evenly—no chaos here.
- In a bowl, whisk together milk, sugar, and vanilla extract until smooth. That's your liquid gold.
- Pour the mixture evenly over the bread and bananas, pressing gently to soak everything.
- Cover and cook on low for 2–3 hours, until the bread is golden and custardy.
- Scoop it out, drizzle some caramel sauce if you're feeling fancy, and garnish with mint. It's dessert time, boss.

RECIPE TIPS

Use slightly stale bread—it soaks up the custard better and avoids sogginess. For extra richness, swap half the milk for cream. If you've got a sweet tooth, sprinkle a little cinnamon-sugar mix on top before cooking. Don't overcook—keep it soft and gooey in the middle. Pair it with coffee or a scoop of ice cream for next-level indulgence. This is dessert done right without breaking a sweat.

Molten Chocolate Fondue

INGREDIENTS

- 4 oz dark chocolate, chopped
- 1/4 cup heavy cream
- 1 tbsp honey or sugar
- 4 strawberries, whole
- 4 marshmallows or cake cubes

THE BENEFITS

Molten Chocolate Fondue brings balance to indulgence. Dark chocolate is rich in antioxidants and minerals, while strawberries add vitamin C and fiber. The small portions of marshmallows or cake satisfy sweet cravings without overloading. Heavy cream adds a touch of richness, making this dessert both luxurious and surprisingly wholesome when shared.

PREPARATION

- Toss the chopped chocolate and heavy cream into your crockpot. Set it on low heat and let it melt gently for about 20–25 minutes.
- Stir in the honey or sugar to sweeten things up as the chocolate melts. Keep stirring every 5–10 minutes to make it smooth and glossy.
- Once the chocolate reaches molten perfection, switch the crockpot to the warm setting to keep it ready for dipping.
- Lay out strawberries, marshmallows, and cake cubes for dunking. Arrange everything while the chocolate stays warm.
- Dig in immediately—this is dessert at its finest. Plan for the whole experience to take 30 minutes max from start to finish. Bonus points if you don't double dip!

RECIPE TIPS

Use quality dark chocolate—it makes all the difference. Stir often so nothing burns or gets clumpy. Keep the crockpot on the warm setting once melted. For a fun twist, toss in a pinch of sea salt or a splash of liqueur. Pair it with crisp apples or pineapple for a refreshing kick. This is about fun and flavor, so don't overthink it. Just grab a fork and enjoy the decadence.

Cinnamon Roll Casserole

INGREDIENTS

- 1 can (8 oz) refrigerated cinnamon rolls
- 1/4 cup whole milk
- 2 large eggs
- 1/2 tsp vanilla extract
- 1/4 tsp ground cinnamon

THE BENEFITS

This Cinnamon Roll Casserole is indulgent comfort food with a balanced twist. Eggs bring protein, and milk adds calcium and creaminess. Using a crockpot means no need for frying or heavy butter layers. It's a sweet treat with a warm, homemade feel, perfect for sharing and satisfying your cravings in moderation.

PREPARATION

- Grease your crockpot and cut the cinnamon rolls into quarters. Spread them evenly at the bottom.
- In a bowl, whisk eggs, milk, vanilla extract, and cinnamon until smooth. This is your custard magic.
- Pour the mixture over the cinnamon roll pieces, making sure everything gets a good soak.
- Set the crockpot to low heat and cook for 2–3 hours or until the casserole is set and golden.
- Drizzle the included icing over the top while it's still warm, and sprinkle with extra cinnamon. Serve it up hot and enjoy!

RECIPE TIPS

Layer those cinnamon rolls evenly to get a perfect soak. Don't skip greasing the crockpot unless you're cool with scraping stuck pieces. For extra gooeyness, drizzle the icing right after cooking while it's warm. Want to mix it up? Add chopped nuts or raisins for a fun twist. This dish screams comfort and pairs perfectly with coffee or a lazy weekend vibe.

Whiskey Caramel Bread Pudding

INGREDIENTS

- 2 cups cubed bread (preferably day-old)
- 1/4 cup granulated sugar
- 1/2 cup whole milk
- 1 large egg
- 2 tbsp whiskey

THE BENEFITS

This dessert combines comfort and indulgence with a balanced touch. Bread provides energy-packed carbs, while milk and egg add protein and calcium. The whiskey adds warmth and depth without overpowering the sweetness. By making it at home, you can control the sugar and booze, crafting a satisfying dessert that hits all the right spots.

PREPARATION

- Toss the bread cubes into your greased crockpot—don't be shy, pile it in.
- Whisk milk, egg, sugar, and whiskey in a bowl until smooth. This is where the magic begins.
- Pour the mixture over the bread, pressing down lightly to make sure every piece gets a soak.
- Set the crockpot to low heat and cook for 2–3 hours, or until the pudding is set and golden.
- Drizzle with whiskey caramel sauce when it's warm, garnish with powdered sugar or mint.

RECIPE TIPS

Use slightly stale bread—it soaks up the custard like a champ. Don't skip greasing the crockpot or you'll lose the crispy bits. Stir halfway if you like even cooking. For extra decadence, toss in raisins or chocolate chips. Serve it warm with a dollop of whipped cream or a scoop of vanilla ice cream to take it to another level. This is dessert for kings, made simple.

Dark Chocolate Stout Cake

INGREDIENTS

- 1/2 cup dark chocolate chips
- 1/4 cup stout beer
- 1/4 cup granulated sugar
- 1 large egg
- 1/4 cup all-purpose flour

THE BENEFITS

Dark chocolate packs a punch of antioxidants, while the stout adds depth and a bit of iron. Eggs provide protein, and the sugar is kept in check for balance. This dessert satisfies your chocolate cravings while being rich and indulgent without excessive guilt. Plus, making it yourself beats store-bought cakes every time.

PREPARATION

- Toss the dark chocolate chips and stout into your crockpot on low heat. Stir every 5 minutes until smooth—this is your chocolate base.
- Beat the egg and sugar together in a bowl until fluffy. Stir in the melted chocolate mixture and mix until combined.
- Fold in the flour gently, keeping it light and airy. Pour the batter into a greased crockpot.
- Cook on low for 2 hours or until the cake is firm but moist.
- Let it cool slightly, then slice it up, and serve with a drizzle of melted chocolate or a dusting of cocoa.

RECIPE TIPS

Go for a bold stout—something rich with coffee or chocolate notes adds to the flavor. Stir the batter gently to keep it airy, and always grease the crockpot well. Check the cake early to avoid overcooking; it should stay moist. Serve it with a scoop of vanilla ice cream or a shot of espresso for extra flair. This dessert is a showstopper that's surprisingly easy to pull off.

Maple Bacon Bourbon Blondies

INGREDIENTS

- 1/2 cup all-purpose flour
- 1/4 cup maple syrup
- 1/4 cup crispy cooked bacon bits
- 1 large egg
- 1 tbsp bourbon

THE BENEFITS

Maple Bacon Bourbon Blondies are indulgent yet balanced. Maple syrup provides natural sweetness with minerals like zinc and manganese. Bacon adds protein and a savory twist, while bourbon enhances the flavor with no added sugar. This treat satisfies cravings with wholesome ingredients, making it a smarter choice for indulgent snacking.

PREPARATION

- Combine maple syrup, bourbon, and egg in a bowl—whisk until smooth. This is your flavor-packed base.
- Stir in the flour gradually, mixing just until combined. Add in most of the bacon bits, saving some for garnish.
- Grease your crockpot and pour the batter in, spreading it out evenly.
- Cook on low heat for 2–3 hours until the edges are set but the center is chewy.
- Let it cool slightly, then cut into squares. Top with reserved bacon bits and drizzle with extra maple syrup for that sweet-and-savory punch.

RECIPE TIPS

Don't overmix the batter—keep it light for the perfect chewy texture. Use quality bourbon for the best flavor payoff. Keep an eye on the cook time; pull it early for gooey blondies or let it firm up for more structure. Sprinkle sea salt on top for an elevated sweet-and-salty kick. Serve warm with ice cream or coffee for a seriously satisfying dessert. This is next-level comfort food that hits all the right notes.

Made in United States
Troutdale, OR
12/14/2024

26597780R00042